LIVING *to* COOK

FAVORITE RECIPES OF JANE CITRON
PITTSBURGH FOOD WRITER AND COOKING TEACHER

Designed by
CPI Creative for Cooking Up A Cure © 2009

Peter Pauper Press, Inc.
202 Mamaroneck Avenue
White Plains, NY 10601
All rights reserved
ISBN 978-1-59359-348-3
Printed in Hong Kong
7 6 5 4 3 2 1

*D*edicated to cooks and food lovers everywhere
who embody what Jane did: tremendous passion,
dedication to quality, never-ending energy,
and a pure love for the culinary arts.

FOREWORD

$\mathscr{M}$y mother spent more of her life in the kitchen than anywhere else in the world. I don't mean to suggest that Jane spent her life in exile behind the swinging door that separated the dining room from the kitchen in her house. Rather, with the support of her husband, Carl, Jane traveled the world and learned from its best chefs while pursuing her passion for cooking and good food.

Jane had to choose from literally thousands of recipes, and she worked on this book, off and on, for several years before her death in 2006. Some of the recipes in this book were shared with students in her cooking classes or published in one of the many articles she wrote during her career as a food writer.

Before you explore the recipes, you may want to know a bit more about Jane's life and career.

If we are who we are through a combination of nature and nurture, there was no question that Jane would find a life in food. Her mother, Lillian Pachtman, was a very good cook and an excellent baker. My mother recalled that one of her early memories was of watching her mother mix crushed Ritz crackers, grated onion, cold water, and ketchup into her meat loaf, which she described as an exquisite introduction to comfort food.

After getting married at age twenty-one—more or less the norm in 1955—Jane began to develop her cooking skills on an extended eighteen-month honeymoon in San Francisco while Carl served his country as a Private First Class in the Army. They returned to Pittsburgh, where Jane taught nursery school and Sunday school and started a family. My brothers Stanley and Alan arrived in 1958 and 1960, respectively, and I showed up in 1966.

As we grew up, our family ate in shifts, except on Sunday nights and special occasions. The children ate early, and our dinners were simple: spaghetti, hamburgers, or, on a special night, roast leg of lamb with mustard-herb coating, served with a green salad and potato gratin.

My brothers and I believed that potatoes, especially potatoes shredded then fried in a pan to a crisp in butter and oil and generously seasoned with salt and pepper, trumped any green vegetable. (I later learned that my mother's fried potatoes were known in the food world as potatoes roesti.)

My mother prepared a second dinner while waiting for my father to return home from the office. They dined on finer fare. To me and my brothers upstairs, watching television and doing homework, the smells were captivating. As the youngest by six years, I occasionally was able to cadge a second supper, perhaps a few pieces of veal scaloppine cooked in white wine sauce with some angel hair pasta on the side.

My mother performed all of the tasks related to cooking when we were growing up. She was a perfectionist who believed it was easier to do the work herself. My brothers and I were responsible for setting the table and drying dishes. Occasionally, we were enlisted in a simple task, such as tailing green beans or peeling potatoes.

Although Jane strived for perfection, by no means was she severe. She enjoyed working in the kitchen and delighted in explaining what she was doing to us and the students in her classes. As an adult, I spent countless hours talking with my mother in her kitchen, comparing notes about the books we were reading, telling her about my work and friends, and watching her perform a task such as chopping onions flawlessly and then cleaning up before moving on to the next undertaking.

In the second half of the 1970s, Stanley departed for the University of Pittsburgh and Alan for Penn State, leaving the nest empty except for me. As she later explained, Jane gave up a mediocre tennis pastime and focused her efforts on becoming a cooking teacher. She started by taking a series of classes with Ferdinand Metz, then working at the H. J. Heinz Company. (Our family still enjoys the Hungarian Goulash with Spaetzle that Metz taught my mother.)

In 1978, Jane began teaching cooking classes in her kitchen. My father and I feasted on practice meals made in preparation for her classes. One night, I returned home from soccer practice and devoured an entire rack of lamb persillade—succulent lamb with a parsley-garlic crumb topping. For several nights in a row, dessert consisted of individual chocolate soufflés that my mother was fine-tuning for her students. I assure you that no other teenager has ever eaten so well.

My mother continued to take cooking classes, some of them in Europe. Jane studied with Madeleine Kamman in Annecy, France, an experience that redefined her approach to cooking. Kamman, an accomplished chef, teacher, and author, emphasized knowledge of food science and mastery of techniques in her intensive two-week course. After a class in 1981, Jane was invited to assist Kamman the next summer. My mother credited this as a turning point in her cooking career. Around this time, Jane also studied with Marcella Hazan in Bologna, met Julie Dannenbaum at the Greenbrier, and took a few classes from Jacques Pépin, later assisting him when he appeared in Pittsburgh.

Back in Pittsburgh, Jane's cooking classes were popular, and, after she was featured in the food section of the local newspaper, she began writing about food for the *Pittsburgh Press*. (During more than twenty years as a food writer, Jane also wrote for the *Pittsburgh Post-Gazette* and *Pittsburgh Magazine* and a number of other publications as a freelance writer.)

Sometimes, my family vacationed together. One such trip was to the French Riviera. I still recall being enthralled by the many cats at Simone Beck's farmhouse, Bramafam, in the South of France. My mother spent the afternoon interviewing Simca, as she was known, for the *Pittsburgh Press*. Simca spoke flawless English as she discussed her life in France, her friendship with Julia Child, and the experience of writing *Mastering the Art of French Cooking* with Child and Louisette Bertholle.

After years of enjoying eating my mother's food and helping with the dishes, I became interested in cooking during my last year of law school. Although I was often clueless in my salad days—I did not know until after my first batch of split pea soup that a recipe calling for a clove of garlic does not require the entire head—I had internalized a very precise sense of taste from growing up on my mother's food.

This collection of Jane's recipes will certainly give you a full sense of her palate. We hope that you will enjoy them as much as her family and students have.

RODGER DANIEL CITRON

Contents

APPETIZERS
2

PIZZAS AND SAVORY PASTRIES
16

EGGS
32

SALADS
38

SOUPS AND STEWS
50

PASTA
66

FISH AND SEAFOOD
74

POULTRY
92

MEAT
104

BREADS AND MUFFINS
122

DESSERTS

PIES
130

CAKES
142

OTHER
159

APPETIZERS

Maytag Blue Stuffed Shrimp
with Red Cocktail Sauce

4

Miniature Tarts
Cheese Soufflé Tarts
Spinach Ricotta Tarts

6-7

Cured Salmon with Fennel Greens
Silver Dollar Corn Cakes
Potato Crisps
Crème Fraîche

8-11

Shrimp Rémoulade

11

Salmon Tartare with Guacamole

13

Salmon Rillettes

14

Fried Zucchini
with Peppered Yogurt Sauce

15

Maytag Blue Stuffed Shrimp with Red Cocktail Sauce

Though my mother did not keep kosher, she never allowed pork, ham, or bacon in our house. But oh how she loved shrimp and crabmeat! When I saw fresh shrimp and crabmeat in the kitchen, I knew company was coming.

Yield: Approximately 15 shrimp

To cook shrimp:

1 pound raw shrimp in the shell (size 10–15 to the pound)
1 tablespoon Old Bay Seasoning

Make lengthwise cut through top of shell and butterfly shrimp by cutting along the vein halfway through shrimp. Remove vein but do not remove shell.

Bring 3 quarts of water to a boil; add Old Bay Seasoning, then shrimp. When water returns to boil, remove pot from heat and let shrimp sit in water 5 minutes, or until firm and white. Prepare an ice bath, drain shrimp in colander, then transfer to ice bath to cool. Remove shell and any remaining vein but not tail shell. Cut along where the vein was to open (butterfly) shrimp. Blot dry and fill.

Filling

4 ounces cream cheese, at room temperature
2 ounces Maytag or other blue cheese of your choice, grated
1 teaspoon grated shallot
1 teaspoon Dijon mustard
½ cup finely minced parsley

Combine cheeses with shallot and Dijon mustard in a bowl and mix well. Using a metal spatula or flat knife, spread cheese mixture evenly into the split backs of the shrimp. Dust cheese with parsley and serve chilled with cocktail sauce.

Between the lines: Cutting through the shrimp shell makes removing the vein easier. Veins should always be removed. Cooking shrimp in the shell protects the shrimp and ensures better texture.

COCKTAIL SAUCE

Yield: Approximately 1½ cups

---

1 bottle Heinz Chili Sauce
Juice of half a lemon
1½ teaspoons Dijon mustard
3–4 tablespoons prepared white horseradish, or more to taste
Generous dash Worcestershire sauce
Tabasco to taste

Combine all ingredients and mix well.

Between the lines: Use any extra cheese mixture to fill celery or endive, or pipe through a pastry tube onto croutons and sprinkle with cut chives.

Miniature Tarts

I have included two of my favorite hors d'oeuvre recipes made from a basic pastry crust. Both fillings and pastry may be assembled ahead, and the pan covered with tinfoil and placed in the freezer until needed. Spinach or cheese, these miniature tarts are delicious, have eye appeal, and are easy to eat.

Yield: Approximately 30–36 servings

Pastry

1½ cups sifted all-purpose flour
¾ teaspoon salt
½ cup solid vegetable shortening
4–5 tablespoons ice water

Mix sifted flour and salt in a bowl. Cut in shortening with a pastry blender until pieces are size of small peas. Sprinkle 2 tablespoons water over mixture and bring together with a fork. Push to one side. Sprinkle enough of the remaining water over dry mixture so that dough can be gathered into a ball.

On a lightly floured surface, flatten dough into a round disk and roll approximately ⅛ inch thick. With a cookie or biscuit cutter, cut rounds to fit the cups of a miniature muffin pan.

Cheese Soufflé Tarts

3 tablespoons butter
3 tablespoons flour
¾ cup milk
Salt, freshly ground pepper, and nutmeg to taste
3 egg yolks
¾ cup coarsely grated Emmenthal cheese
½ cup grated or crumbled young goat cheese (soft)
4 egg whites
Dash of salt and cream of tartar

Melt butter in a saucepan and add flour, stirring to combine. Cook a few minutes, then whisk in milk and stir until mixture comes to a boil. Lower heat and simmer 2 to 3 minutes. Season with salt, pepper, and nutmeg. Off the heat, beat in egg yolks one at a time, combining well after each addition. Add cheeses, return to heat, and over low heat, cook only until cheese melts.

Beat egg whites with salt and cream of tartar until stiff but not dry. Beat one-quarter of the mixture into the soufflé base to lighten it, and then gently fold in remaining whites.

Preheat oven to 400 degrees. Fill pastry-lined muffin cups with cheese soufflé to the top and bake in a hot oven approximately 12 to 15 minutes, or until soufflé has puffed and pastry has lightly browned.

Spinach Ricotta Tarts

---

4 strips thick-sliced bacon
1 tablespoon butter
2 small cloves garlic, pressed
2 shallots, minced
1 10-ounce package fresh spinach or 1 package frozen leaf spinach, thawed
1 cup ricotta cheese
Salt and freshly ground pepper
Dash nutmeg

Dice bacon and sauté until crisp. Drain and reserve bacon bits. Pour fat from pan, add butter, and when hot, sauté garlic and shallots until soft. Do not brown. Add spinach, cover, and cook until spinach wilts. Place in processor or blender and puree until smooth. Add ricotta cheese and process only until smooth. Season with salt, pepper, and nutmeg. Mix in bacon bits.

Preheat oven to 400 degrees. Fill pastry-lined miniature muffin cups with spinach mixture and bake 10 to 12 minutes, until slightly puffed and pastry has lightly browned.

CURED SALMON WITH FENNEL GREENS

*T*his multipurpose recipe uses salt-cured salmon (gravlax), mimicking the flavor and texture of premium smoked salmon. Serve with Silver Dollar Corn Cakes or Potato Crisps, or for Sunday brunch on a toasted bagel garnished with thinly sliced onion and cucumber.

The concept of curing salmon with salt, sugar, and spices originated in Scandinavia, but Chef Bradley Ogden put a new spin on the recipe by using fennel greens instead of dill in a class several years ago at Fetzer Vineyards in Hopland, California. The recipe has been a favorite ever since.

Yield: About 48 generous hors d'oeuvres

---

2 tablespoons cracked black peppercorns
2 tablespoons cracked white peppercorns
4 tablespoons kosher salt
4 tablespoons sugar
1 side of salmon, skin left on (about 2 pounds), edges trimmed and bones removed
2 large bunches fresh fennel (feathery greens only)

Combine seasonings and mix well. Place salmon, skin side up, on a large piece of cheesecloth and spread half of the seasonings on skin side of fish. Top with 1 bunch of fennel greens. Turn salmon over and top flesh side with remaining seasoning and fennel. Fennel greens should completely cover fish.

Wrap cheesecloth over salmon and place in a shallow pan or on a platter and place a heavy weight—bricks work well—on top. Cure in the refrigerator for at least 3 days and as long as 5, turning salmon daily and draining off any excess liquid from the salmon.

Remove seasonings, slice very thin, and serve with Silver Dollar Corn Cakes or Potato Crisps.

Between the lines: Consider investing in a professional slicing knife to make slicing the salmon easier. It allows you to cut paper-thin slices like a chef. Slice on the diagonal.

Silver Dollar Corn Cakes

Yield: Approximately 30–36 small corn cakes

1½ cups corn kernels, preferably fresh (3 ears of corn)
½ cup milk
⅓ cup cornmeal
½–¾ cup flour
4 tablespoons unsalted butter, melted
2 whole eggs
2 egg yolks
Salt and freshly ground pepper
Clarified butter or vegetable oil
Crème Fraîche or sour cream
Slices of thinly sliced salmon
3–4 tablespoons snipped chives

Remove corn from cob, place kernels in a food processor, and process until corn has a chunky but creamy consistency. Add milk, cornmeal, and ½ cup flour, and process into a smooth batter without lumps. Add melted butter, whole eggs and egg yolks, and salt and pepper to processor and pulse two or three times to blend. Pour batter into a bowl. Batter should loosely hold its shape. If too thin, whisk in some additional flour. Cover loosely with foil and allow batter to rest 1 hour before using.

Heat a large nonstick sauté pan over medium-high heat. Brush with enough clarified butter or oil to cover bottom of pan. Pour in batter to make pancakes the size of silver dollars. Cook 2 minutes, or until golden brown, then flip. Cook for 2 more minutes. Drain on paper towels. Repeat with remaining batter. When necessary, repeat brushing of pan with clarified butter.

Serve three pancakes per serving. Arrange pancakes and salmon on a plate, garnish each pancake with a dollop of Crème Fraîche, and top with a sprinkling of chives.

To clarify butter: Melt butter over very low heat. Remove foam from top and pour off clear liquid, discarding milk solids on the bottom. Though it is not mandatory to refrigerate clarified butter, I prefer keeping it in the refrigerator.

Between the lines: This batter freezes very well.

POTATO CRISPS

At the Mandarin Oriental Hotel in San Francisco, Chef Howard Bulka introduced my husband and me to these marvelous Potato Crisps, which are easy to make and even easier to eat. Potato Crisps pair beautifully with smoked salmon or caviar, garnished with a dollop of Crème Fraîche and chives.

Yield: 6–8 servings

3–4 medium-sized baking potatoes
Salt and freshly ground pepper
3–4 tablespoons corn or canola oil

Scrub potato skins but do not peel. Grate on the coarse side of a square hand-grater. Season with salt and pepper and wring out excess moisture. This is best done with your hands.

In a large nonstick frying pan, heat oil over medium-high heat. Form potato rounds approximately 2 inches in diameter and place in pan, flattening tops with a metal spatula. Sauté until bottoms are crisp, then turn and crisp second side. Drain on paper towels, salt lightly, and serve.

When making large quantities of Potato Crisps, you may prepare them ahead and reheat in the oven or serve at room temperature.

Between the lines: If I were asked to name my favorite herb, I would answer chives. A sprinkling of chives adds elegance to cream soups, works as a garnish, and may be used in salads, omelettes, and appetizers. Cut chives with a small, sharp knife.

CRÈME FRAÎCHE

Crème Fraîche, a staple in France, is easily made and may be used in cooking or as a dessert topping or garnish. Use fresh cream that is not ultrapasteurized, and the best-quality cream available, with the highest butterfat.

Yield: 1¼ cups

1 cup heavy cream
⅓ cup buttermilk

Combine heavy cream and buttermilk in a jar. Blend well but do not shake. Close jar.
Allow mixture to sit at room temperature until cream is consistency of loose Jell-O.
This can take anywhere from 6 to 24 hours, depending on how warm your kitchen is.
Refrigerate 6 hours before using.

SHRIMP RÉMOULADE

In 1960, my husband, Carl, and I took our first trip to New Orleans. We dined at
Antoine's, Galatoire's, and Arnaud's, and had breakfast at Brennan's and beignets and
coffee with chicory every morning. We tried many new and exciting dishes, the most
memorable being Oysters Rockefeller and Shrimp Rémoulade. Right then and there
we decided, next stop Europe.

Yield: Approximately 6–8 appetizer servings

RÉMOULADE SAUCE

1 egg yolk
2 tablespoons Dijon or Creole mustard
½ cup extra-virgin olive oil
1 tablespoon white wine vinegar
2 teaspoons paprika
1½ tablespoons prepared horseradish
1 teaspoon minced garlic
¼ cup finely chopped scallions (white parts and tender green tops)
¼ cup finely chopped celery
2 tablespoons finely chopped parsley
2–3 tablespoons chili sauce (Heinz preferred)
Tabasco and salt to taste

Place egg yolk and mustard in a small bowl. Whisk with a wire whisk and slowly add oil,
whisking briskly to make a mayonnaise. Add remaining ingredients and mix well.

continued

1 pound raw shrimp in the shell
1 teaspoon Old Bay Seasoning (optional)
Salt to taste
A blend of romaine lettuce hearts and radicchio (3 parts romaine, 1 part radicchio),
    to make 4–5 cups, cut in chiffonade*

*The French cooking term *chiffonade* means to cut into fine strips. Stack leaves of romaine, roll lengthwise into a tight roll, and cut horizontally into thin strips. Repeat with radicchio.

To cook shrimp: Split shrimp shells with a small, sharp-pointed knife or scissors along the top and remove vein but not the shell. Bring a large pot of water to boil and add salt, and if desired, Old Bay Seasoning. Add shrimp in shells, and when water returns to a boil, turn off heat and allow shrimp to remain in water 10 minutes. Then drain under cold water and remove shells. Blot dry and cool completely.

Combine shrimp with enough sauce to coat well. Turn into a bowl and refrigerate 2 hours, or until serving time.

To serve: Place romaine lettuce and radicchio chiffonade on a serving platter and arrange shrimp on top, finishing with any remaining sauce.

Salmon Tartare with Guacamole

*S*almon Tartare with Guacamole was inspired by Chef Thomas Keller's marvelous signature amuse, "Coronets"—Salmon Tartare with Sweet Red Onion Crème Fraîche, served in a tiny, savory cone. I met Thomas Keller the first year he opened in Yountville, California, and through the years, he became a friend.

Yield: About 1½ cups

½ pound fresh salmon, belly preferred, skin and any small bones removed
2–3 teaspoons extra-virgin olive oil
Grated rind of 1 large lemon, or a few drops of lemon oil
3 teaspoons minced shallots
Salt and freshly ground white pepper to taste
Guacamole (see recipe)
Crème Fraîche (p. 10)
Snipped chives
Toasts or crispy Asian-type crackers or lavosh

With a sharp knife, finely mince the salmon fillet. Do not use a food processor. Place minced salmon in a small bowl and stir in the remaining ingredients. Adjust seasoning and refrigerate the tartare for at least 30 minutes or up to 12 hours.

Guacamole

2 large avocados
3 tablespoons lime or lemon juice, or a combination
1 small onion, grated
2 small green chile peppers, chopped fine (about 2 tablespoons), or to taste
1 small clove garlic, minced or pressed
1 tomato, peeled, seeded, and chopped (about ½ cup)
Salt to taste
1 tablespoon mayonnaise (optional)

Peel and seed avocados. Place in a small bowl and mash with a fork. Add juice, onion, green chile peppers, garlic, tomato, and salt. Mix well. Depending on the consistency of the mixture, you may wish to add a small amount of mayonnaise for creaminess.

Spread Salmon Tartare on small toasts, crispy Asian crackers, or lavosh and top with a dollop of Guacamole, a dab of Crème Fraîche, and a sprinkling of snipped chives.

Salmon Rillettes

In bistros, rillettes may be made with a mix of pork or salmon and are served with crusty bread, some mustard, and perhaps a few cornichons. Use as an appetizer, lunch dish, or canapé, make into a salad by serving with baby greens and herbs, or even spread on a toasted bagel for breakfast. Here is an easy-to-do recipe to serve a multitude of occasions.

Yield: About 2 cups

½ pound salmon, poached in ½ cup dry white wine
½ pound smoked salmon, diced
8 ounces cream cheese, softened
1 tablespoon vodka
Salt, freshly ground pepper, and cayenne to taste
2 tablespoons snipped chives or dill
Thinly sliced cucumber rounds
Belgian endive leaves

Place salmon in small frying pan with wine. Cover with a round of buttered wax paper, bring to a boil, lower heat, and simmer until salmon is cooked but still very moist, about 5 to 7 minutes, depending on thickness of fish. Remove pan from heat and cool salmon in liquid. Transfer salmon to a board and discard skin and any bones, then flake the fish into small pieces.

Place smoked salmon, cream cheese, and vodka in the bowl of a food processor and process until smooth. Transfer contents to a medium-size bowl and add salt, freshly ground pepper, cayenne, and chives or dill. With a fork, work in flaked salmon until mixture is blended.

The finished rillettes may be served from a crock with toast points or crackers, or piped through a pastry tube onto cucumber rounds or into Belgian endive leaves.

This mixture freezes well.

Between the lines: When buying fresh salmon, I avoid farm-raised, which lacks both taste and texture. Try to buy wild salmon or a seasonal product. In buying smoked salmon, I opt for a whole side of salmon. I would rather do my own slicing at home with a proper knife.

FRIED ZUCCHINI WITH PEPPERED YOGURT SAUCE

*W*hen I serve Fried Zucchini, guests just about lick the platter clean. Sometimes I gussy up the dip by using a sauce made with Crème Fraîche, Dijon mustard, a touch of tomato paste, chopped basil, and snipped chives.

Yield: 6–8 appetizer servings

1 pound zucchini
Approximately ⅔ cup all-purpose flour, or enough to make a coating batter
1 cup water
Salt to taste
Vegetable oil, enough to come up ¾ inch on the side of frying pan

Wash the zucchini and cut each one into 2½ to 3-inch chunks. Slice chunks lengthwise into thin slices ⅛ inch thick. Salt slices and drain for 20 minutes. Pat dry.

Pour water into a shallow dish and, using a sifter, gradually add the flour, whisking the mixture to blend. Add salt to taste. Batter should have consistency of loose sour cream; if necessary, add more flour to thicken, or thin with water. Add zucchini to batter and coat pieces evenly.

Heat oil until hot but not smoking. Slip in only as many zucchini as will fit comfortably in the pan. Do not crowd. When golden crust has formed, turn and brown second side. Drain on paper towel and salt lightly. Serve immediately with yogurt sauce.

YOGURT SAUCE

1 cup plain yogurt
Seasoned pepper to taste (Lawry's preferred)

Mix yogurt to blend in a small bowl and top with seasoned pepper.

PIZZAS AND SAVORY PASTRIES

Mario's White Pizza
18

Pizza Dough
18

Pizza Margherita
19

Pizza Pepe
20

Pizza with Caramelized Onions, Walnuts, Gorgonzola, and Mozzarella Cheese
21

Pizza with Escarole, Roasted Tomatoes, and Cheese
22

Pizza with Porcini and Fresh Mushrooms
23

Alsatian Onion Tart
Pâte Brisée Pastry Crust
24–26

Pissaladière
26

Tomato and Roasted Red Pepper Tart
28

Spanakopita
30

Tourte aux Blettes
31

Mario's White Pizza

1 packaged 12-inch pizza shell (such as Boboli)
2 tablespoons olive oil
1 tablespoon (heaping) minced garlic
2 tablespoons (or more) chopped fresh basil
2 medium-sized tomatoes, thinly sliced
½–¾ pound grated cheese (combination of mozzarella and provolone)
¼ cup grated Romano or Parmesan cheese
2 teaspoons dried oregano

Preheat oven to 425 degrees. Brush crust with olive oil and sprinkle with garlic and basil. Arrange tomato slices over crust and top with grated cheeses. Bake 12 to 15 minutes, or until cheese has melted and crust is lightly browned. Sprinkle with oregano.

Pizza Dough

Yield: Two 10-inch pizzas

1 cup lukewarm water
2 teaspoons active dry yeast
1 teaspoon sugar
¼ cup extra-virgin olive oil, plus more to oil bowl
2 teaspoons salt
3 cups unbleached all-purpose flour, approximately
Cornmeal for sprinkling on parchment or pizza paddle

Pour the warm water into a large bowl, sprinkle the yeast into the water, stir in sugar, and proof mixture 8 to 10 minutes, or until foamy. Add ¼ cup olive oil and salt, then gradually stir in approximately 3 cups of flour, or as needed to form a dough firm enough to knead.

Turn onto a lightly floured surface and knead dough until smooth and elastic, about 5 minutes. If dough feels too soft or sticky, sprinkle small amounts of flour over the dough or onto the work surface.

Lightly oil a large bowl with olive oil. Place dough in bowl and turn in bowl to coat with oil. Cover with plastic wrap and let dough rise in a warm place until it has doubled, approximately 1 to 1½ hours. Punch down and divide dough into two pieces and roll out on a lightly floured board according to recipe directions.

Dough freezes well.

Pizza Margherita

Yield: Two 10-inch pizzas

Olive oil as needed
2 cups fresh tomatoes, peeled, seeded, and chopped
2 tablespoons tomato paste or sauce, if needed for thicker sauce
Salt and freshly ground pepper to taste
1 cup chopped fresh basil, divided
1 recipe Pizza Dough (p. 18)
Garlic-flavored olive oil (3 tablespoons olive oil combined with 2 teaspoons minced
    garlic), optional
1½ cups diced mozzarella mixed with 1 tablespoon olive oil, divided
½ cup freshly grated Parmesan cheese, divided

Heat 2 tablespoons olive oil in a small skillet. Add tomatoes and cook 3 to 4 minutes over moderately high heat. Add tomato paste, if desired. Season with salt and pepper. Drain in a strainer 30 minutes. Basil may be added to tomatoes at this point or sprinkled over them when on pizza dough.

Preheat oven to 425 degrees. If using tiles or a pizza stone, preheat oven for at least 30 minutes.

Divide dough into two pieces. On a floured board, roll one piece into a 10-inch circle. If desired, brush round lightly with garlic-flavored olive oil. Cover dough with half of mozzarella cheese, then add tomatoes. Sprinkle with half of Parmesan cheese.

Bake about 15 minutes, or until crust is lightly browned and cheese melted. Repeat directions with second pizza.

Note: It is best to slide pizza directly onto tiles or pizza stone in your oven with a pizza paddle sprinkled with cornmeal. If you feel more comfortable, bake on parchment paper.

Pizza Pepe

Yield: Two 10-inch pizzas

½ cup water
½ cup dry white wine
2 crushed garlic cloves
1 bouquet garni (sprig parsley, thyme, and bay leaf)
2 dozen clams
1 small (7½ ounce) can chopped clams
2 teaspoons oregano
½ cup chopped flat-leaf parsley
¼ cup heavy cream
Cornstarch slurry (2 tablespoons cornstarch dissolved in 3 tablespoons cold water)
¼ cup olive oil
3 cloves garlic, minced
8–10 slices thick bacon, cut into 1½-inch squares
1 recipe Pizza Dough (p. 18)

In a pot, combine water, wine, garlic, and bouquet garni. Add clams, cover, and bring to a boil. Lower heat to medium and steam clams until they open, then remove to side dish. If clams are large, cut into bite-size pieces. Strain liquid through cheesecloth or strainer lined with wet paper towel and reserve.

Combine reserved liquid with 1 can chopped clams. Add oregano and 2 tablespoons from the ½ cup of flat-leaf parsley and simmer 5 minutes. Add cream and thicken by gradually adding cornstarch slurry to simmering liquid.

Combine olive oil and minced garlic and reserve. Partially cook bacon slices in a frying pan 4 to 5 minutes until soft but not brown, and reserve.

Preheat oven to 425 degrees and baking tiles or a pizza stone for 30 minutes.

Divide dough into two pieces; roll out first half on a floured surface. Transfer to pizza paddle to finish rolling and form a 9 to 10-inch circle.

Brush crust with garlic oil, then brush or spoon enough sauce over top to make a thin layer. Dot crust with half of reserved clams and half of bacon slices. Bake 15 minutes, or until sauce is bubbling and crust is golden. Sprinkle with half of the remaining parsley and serve. Repeat directions for second pizza.

Pizza with Caramelized Onions, Walnuts, Gorgonzola, and Mozzarella Cheese

Yield: Two 10-inch pizzas

Olive oil as needed
4–5 cups thinly sliced onions
Salt and freshly ground pepper
Pinch of sugar
1 recipe Pizza Dough (p. 18)
Cornmeal as needed (for pizza paddle)
1½ cups grated Gorgonzola cheese
1½ cups grated mozzarella cheese
½ cup coarsely chopped walnuts (optional)
1 red bell pepper, thinly sliced into rounds (optional)
½ cup chopped parsley

Heat 3 to 4 tablespoons olive oil in a large frying pan and sauté onions over low heat. Season with salt and freshly ground pepper. Cook slowly, until brown. A pinch of sugar speeds up the process.

Preheat oven to 425 degrees and place tiles or pizza baking stone inside. Preheat for at least 30 minutes.

Divide dough into two rounds. Cover one round and roll second round of dough on a floured board until approximately 12 inches in diameter. Sprinkle pizza paddle lightly with cornmeal and transfer pizza to paddle. Spread half of the onions over the dough, and sprinkle with half of the cheeses and walnuts. If desired, garnish with a few thinly sliced red pepper rings. Transfer pizza from paddle to oven tiles and bake approximately 15 minutes, until cheeses have melted and crust is lightly browned. Sprinkle with half of parsley, cut into wedges, and serve. Repeat procedure with second round of dough.

Pizza with Escarole, Roasted Tomatoes, and Cheese

Yield: Two 10-inch pizzas

To roast tomatoes:

1-2 pounds fresh plum tomatoes
Salt
Olive oil

Heat oven to warm (about 180 degrees; no warmer than 200 degrees). Cut plum tomatoes in half and arrange on a baking sheet, cutting a small slice from any halves that will not stand. Season tomato halves with salt and sprinkle with a few drops of olive oil. Roast tomatoes 6 to 8 hours. When cool enough to handle, remove skin. Store well covered in the refrigerator. Shelf life is 5 to 6 days.

2–3 tablespoons olive oil
¼ cup finely chopped shallots or onions
1 tablespoon minced garlic
2½ cups chopped escarole
⅓ cup roasted red or yellow bell pepper, cut into julienne
1 recipe Pizza Dough (p. 18)
Enough cornmeal to sprinkle lightly over pizza paddle
Garlic flavored oil (3 tablespoons olive oil combined with 2 teaspoons minced garlic)
¾ cup coarsely grated mozzarella cheese
1 cup chopped roasted plum tomatoes
1 cup grated Asiago or Fontina cheese
½ cup grated Parmesan cheese (optional)

Filling may be made ahead and pizzas assembled right before baking. Heat olive oil in a sauté pan, add shallots, and cook 3 minutes until soft. Add garlic and cook an additional 30 seconds. Add escarole and cook, stirring occasionally, until wilted. Mix in red or yellow roasted peppers.

Divide pizza dough in half. Roll out one half on a floured board to make a circle approximately 10 to 12 inches in diameter. Brush with half of garlic-flavored oil. Place crust on a pizza paddle sprinkled with cornmeal.

Arrange half of the escarole mixture on first pizza. Sprinkle half of the mozzarella on top; add half of the roasted tomatoes, finishing with half of the Asiago cheese and a sprinkling of Parmesan if desired. Repeat for second pizza.

Preheat oven to 425 degrees. If using tiles or pizza stone, bake pizza directly on tiles. This is done with a pizza paddle sprinkled lightly with cornmeal to move pizza in and out of the oven. Bake pizza until cheese has melted and crust is lightly browned, about 15 minutes.

Note: When using tiles or pizza stone, preheat oven at least 30 minutes.

PIZZA WITH PORCINI AND FRESH MUSHROOMS

Yield: Two 10-inch pizzas

1 ounce dried porcini mushrooms, soaked in 1½–2 cups hot water for 20 minutes
3 tablespoons extra-virgin olive oil
¾ pound fresh button mushrooms
 Reserved porcini soaking liquid
3 tablespoons extra-virgin olive oil
2 cloves garlic, pressed or minced
1 recipe Pizza Dough (p. 18)
Flour and cornmeal
3 cups Italian cheese (Tartufo Nero, Montasio, used alone or
   in combination with mozzarella), grated or cut into small dice
1 cup freshly grated Parmigiano-Reggiano cheese
White truffle oil (optional)
Finely chopped parsley or chives
Pizza stone and pizza paddle

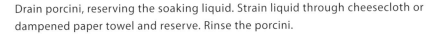

Drain porcini, reserving the soaking liquid. Strain liquid through cheesecloth or dampened paper towel and reserve. Rinse the porcini.

Heat olive oil in a medium to large frying pan and, when hot, add porcini and button mushrooms and sauté over medium heat 3 to 4 minutes. Strain mushrooms, reserving any juices. Add the reserved porcini soaking liquid to juices from the cooked mushrooms in the unwashed frying pan and reduce over medium heat to ¼ cup. Combine with cooked mushrooms in a small bowl. Combine olive oil and pressed or minced garlic and set aside.

Preheat pizza stone in 425-degree oven for 30 minutes.

continued

On a wooden board, roll or stretch dough into two 10-inch rounds, adding flour to board if dough should become sticky. Sprinkle cornmeal over pizza paddle, transfer pizza dough to pan, and, if necessary, finish rolling into rounds. Brush crust with garlic oil. Arrange half of mushrooms, half of diced or grated cheese, and half of grated Parmigiano-Reggiano on each round.

Transfer from pizza paddle to pizza stone and bake 15 minutes.

With a sharp knife cut into pieces, and finish with sprinkling of white truffle oil, if desired, and finely chopped parsley or chives.

ALSATIAN ONION TART

Onion Tart from Alsace is an excellent example of fine French cooking. The recipe is straightforward and the pastry crust may be made in advance. It is important to remember to prepare the Fromage Blanc far enough ahead to allow it to rest for 24 hours in the refrigerator. Since Whole Foods came to Pittsburgh, you may choose to buy pint containers of Fromage Blanc, which can alleviate any last-minute panic.

Yield: 10 servings

1 recipe Pâte Brisée (recipe follows), rolled ⅛ inch thick to fit 11½-inch tart pan
2 tablespoons butter
1 tablespoon vegetable oil
3 large onions, sliced (about 10 cups, loosely packed)
¼ cup water
3 eggs
1 cup Fromage Blanc
½ cup heavy cream
Salt and freshly ground pepper
Pinch grated nutmeg to taste

TO PREPARE FROMAGE BLANC:

Combine equal parts plain yogurt and low-fat ricotta cheese. Pass through a fine strainer and let rest in refrigerator 24 hours before using.

Heat oil and butter in a large nonstick frying pan, add onions, and cook slowly over low heat until onions are soft and begin to brown, about 20 minutes. Add water and cook an additional 10 minutes, until onions are lightly browned and caramelized.

Preheat oven to 400 degrees.

Beat eggs in a large bowl, then combine with Fromage Blanc and cream, whisking until smooth. Season with salt, pepper, and nutmeg. Add cooked onions and mix well. Pour mixture into prepared pastry shell and bake 45 to 50 minutes, until crust is browned and filling has lightly browned and puffed.

Allow tart to rest 15 to 20 minutes before cutting. Serve at room temperature.

PÂTE BRISÉE PASTRY CRUST

For many years, I avoided using the food processor when making a pastry crust. Even now, I make my mother's original "Crisco" crust by hand. In class, students would tell me how they used the processor for "everything"—pasta, piecrust, pizza. I maintained my stand, but one day I tried the Pâte Brisée in the food processor—and became a believer. Not only did I save time, but I avoided excess handling of the dough, which makes a heavy crust. You are never too old to learn!

Yield: One 11½-inch tart shell

1¼ cups sifted unbleached all-purpose flour
½ teaspoon salt
¼ pound (1 stick) chilled unsalted butter, cut in small cubes
3–4 tablespoons ice water

Combine flour and salt in the bowl of a food processor. Add butter cubes and pulse the machine 12 to 15 times, or until the butter is coated with flour and forms particles the size of peas and resembles very rough sand.

continued

With the motor running, add 3 tablespoons water. Stop processing before the dough forms a ball. Turn dough onto a floured surface, and if very dry, add a little more water. Form into a ball by taking the dough in one hand; using the dough ball as a mop, gather the loose particles on the counter.

With your wrist flat on the counter, extend your hand upward at a 45-degree angle and with the heel of your hand, slide the dough 6 to 8 inches forward only. When all the dough has been used, re-form into a ball and repeat the operation. Flatten dough into a disk, wrap in wax paper, and refrigerate 30 minutes before using.

Flatten dough with a rolling pin and roll on a lightly floured board or cloth to ⅛ inch thick. Fold dough in half, lift carefully, and fit dough into tart pan, trimming excess dough from around the rim, leaving about ½ inch hanging over. Turn crust under and level top rim with a rolling pin or your fingers.

At this point, crust may be filled and baked, or lined with foil, filled with dried beans, and prebaked to be used as a baked shell. When baking a shell, bake 10 minutes in a preheated 450-degree oven, lower heat to 400 degrees, remove foil and beans, and bake 10 minutes more, or until golden.

PISSALADIÈRE

Yield: 8–10 servings

DOUGH

½ package active dry yeast (about 1⅛ teaspoons)
⅓ cup lukewarm water
Pinch of sugar
1½ cups unbleached all-purpose flour
1 egg, beaten
¾ teaspoon salt

Sprinkle yeast over lukewarm water, add sugar, and let stand 5 minutes, until foamy. Pour flour onto a board or into a bowl, make a well in the center, and put dissolved yeast, egg, and salt into well, blending with a fork. Work flour into mixture, mixing to form a dough. The dough should be soft but not sticky. Add more flour if needed.

Turn onto a floured surface and knead dough until elastic and very smooth, about 5 minutes. Transfer dough to an oiled bowl and cover with plastic wrap. Place in a warm area and let rise about 1 hour.

FILLING

6 tablespoons olive oil
2 pounds yellow onions, sliced thin
Pinch of sugar
Salt and freshly ground pepper
1 small can anchovy fillets, soaked in 2 tablespoons milk for 10 minutes, then drained
½ cup halved and pitted oil-cured black olives

Heat oil in a large, heavy frying pan. Add onions and cook slowly over low heat until onions are soft and lightly colored but not brown. Add a pinch of sugar, and cook, covered, for 10 minutes or so. Stir from time to time. Cooking time is approximately 30 to 35 minutes. Season lightly with salt and pepper.

Punch down the dough and roll into a circle to fit an oiled 11-inch tart pan. Press dough into pan to line the bottom and sides.

Spread onions over dough and decorate with the anchovies and olives, making a lattice pattern. Sprinkle with pepper. Leave to rise in a warm place for about 15 minutes while you preheat the oven to 375 degrees.

Bake 25 to 30 minutes, until crust is browned. Serve warm or at room temperature.

Tomato and Roasted Red Pepper Tart

Yield: 8–10 servings

Crust

½ package active dry yeast (1⅛ teaspoons)
⅓ cup lukewarm water
Pinch of sugar
1½ cups unbleached all-purpose flour
1 egg, beaten with ¾ teaspoon salt

In a small bowl, sprinkle yeast over lukewarm water. Add sugar and let sit 5 minutes, until foamy. Place flour in bowl or on board, make a well in the center, and add dissolved yeast and beaten egg. Gradually incorporate flour into egg mixture with a fork until dough can be formed with your hands. If the dough seems too soft, add more flour. Turn dough onto a floured surface and knead until elastic and very smooth, about 5 minutes. Transfer to oiled bowl, cover, and allow to rise in a warm place until doubled, 45 minutes to 1 hour.

Punch dough down on floured board and roll or stretch to fit a lightly oiled 11½-inch tart pan. Set aside for 1 hour.

Filling

3–4 tablespoons olive oil
1 cup onions, chopped
3 cloves garlic, minced
1 cup finely chopped tomatoes (4 medium tomatoes)
1 tablespoon tomato paste
Salt and freshly ground pepper
Dash sugar
Large pinch saffron
Bouquet garni made with thyme sprigs, parsley stems, bay leaf, and tarragon
2 large red bell peppers, roasted (see p. 29)
¼ cup oil-cured black olives, pitted and cut into quarters
Egg wash (1 egg yolk mixed with 1 tablespoon milk)

Heat olive oil in a large frying pan. Add onions and cook over medium heat, stirring often, until golden, about 10 minutes. Add garlic and cook an additional minute or two. Add tomatoes and tomato paste, mixing well. Season with salt and pepper, add sugar, saffron, and bouquet garni, and simmer, covered, over medium-low heat, stirring occasionally, until most of liquid has evaporated and sauce is thick, about 20 minutes.

To bake: Preheat oven to 425 degrees. Spread tomato mixture evenly over the surface of dough. Cut red peppers into thin strips and arrange on top of tomato mixture to make a lattice pattern. Place piece of olive in the center of each square. Brush rim of dough with egg wash and bake until tart is lightly browned and cooked through, about 25 minutes.

To roast peppers: Roast directly over a gas flame or under the broiler, cooking until blistered all over. Turn peppers frequently. When done, place peppers in paper bag and steam for 10 minutes to soften skin, then peel and remove core, seeds, and veins. Alternately, peppers may be baked on a baking sheet in a 350-degree oven, until skins soften, about 30 minutes.

Spanakopita

Yield: 10–12 servings

¼ cup olive oil
½ cup finely chopped onions
½ cup finely chopped scallions
2 pounds fresh spinach, washed, dried, and finely chopped
¼ cup fresh dill weed
½ cup chopped flat-leaf parsley
Salt and freshly ground pepper
½ pound feta cheese, passed through food mill
½ pound ricotta cheese
6 eggs, lightly beaten
2 tablespoons farina
¼ pound (1 stick) unsalted butter, melted, plus more if needed
16 phyllo leaves

In a large heavy skillet, heat olive oil over medium heat until hot. Add the onions and scallions, and cook, stirring often, until soft but not brown. Stir in the spinach, cover, and cook for 5 minutes. Add dill and parsley, season with salt and pepper, and cook, uncovered, for about 10 minutes, or until most of the liquid has evaporated. Transfer to a deep bowl and cool to room temperature.

Combine feta and ricotta cheeses. Add to cooled spinach and blend well. Beat in the eggs, combining mixture well. Add farina, blend well. Adjust seasoning.

Preheat oven to 350 degrees. With a pastry brush, coat the bottom of a 9x13x2-inch baking dish with melted butter. Line the dish with a sheet of phyllo, pressing the edge of the pastry firmly into corners of the dish. Brush surface of pastry with melted butter, spreading to the outside edges. Lay another sheet of phyllo on top. Brush with butter and continue construction until you have eight layers.

With a rubber spatula, spread spinach mixture evenly over the last layer. Smooth into corners, then place another sheet of phyllo on top, brush with butter, and repeat with remaining seven sheets. Trim excess pastry from the rim, turn crust under, and brush the top with butter. Bake in the middle of the oven for 50 to 60 minutes, or until the pastry is crisp and delicately browned. Cut into squares and serve warm or at room temperature.

Tourte aux Blettes

Tourte aux Blettes, or Swiss chard tart, can be found in the bakeries of Nice. What makes this pastry so unusual and "Niçoise" is that the dough is made with olive oil. The tourte may be served as an appetizer or first course, or a savory starch to accompany a main course. I loved the tourte the first time I tasted it on the street in Nice. Ever since, Tourte aux Blettes has been part of my kitchen repertoire.

Yield: 8 servings

Pastry

2 cups unbleached all-purpose flour
1 teaspoon salt
½ cup water
½ scant cup extra-virgin olive oil

Filling

1 bunch Swiss chard leaves
10–12 ounces fresh spinach
3 tablespoons extra-virgin olive oil
½ cup finely chopped onion
Salt and pepper to taste
6 large eggs
1 cup freshly grated Parmesan cheese

Preheat oven to 400 degrees.

Combine flour and salt in a medium-size bowl. Stir in water; add extra-virgin olive oil, mixing until well blended. Knead briefly. Press or roll dough to fit a 10½-inch metal tart tin with removable bottom. Wash and spin-dry the green leafy portion of chard, removing center stems. Repeat with spinach, removing stems. Chop leaves. In a skillet, heat 3 tablespoons olive oil and sauté onion until soft. Add chard and spinach over low heat, and cook until leaves have wilted. Season with salt and pepper.

Combine the eggs by whisking, then add cheese and blend well. Stir in chard-spinach mixture. When ready to bake, pour filling into prepared tin. Bake until crust is golden and filling firm and browned, about 40 minutes.

EGGS

ASPARAGUS CHEESE SOUFFLÉ
34

THAI OMELET
36

NEW JOE'S SPECIAL
37

Asparagus Cheese Soufflé

This recipe makes a lovely luncheon entrée and, with a can of asparagus on hand, may be easily and quickly prepared. A favorite cheese of your choice may be substituted for the Gruyère. I like the addition of Parmesan cheese for taste and texture.

Yield: 4–6 servings

Prepare the soufflé dish:

1 tablespoon unsalted butter
3 tablespoons grated Parmesan cheese (preferably Parmigiano-Reggiano)

Butter a 1½-quart soufflé dish and sprinkle inside with the Parmesan cheese. Set aside.

Soufflé:

3 tablespoons unsalted butter
3 tablespoons flour
¾ cup milk
¾ cup grated Gruyère cheese
3 egg yolks
1 cup chopped canned or fresh yellow-white asparagus (If using canned asparagus, drain off liquid. If using fresh asparagus, trim, peel, and blanch in boiling salted water for 1 to 2 minutes. Refresh under cold water, drain, and dry on paper towels.)
½ teaspoon salt
Freshly ground pepper
Dash grated nutmeg
Dash cayenne pepper
4–5 egg whites
Dash salt
¼ teaspoon cream of tartar

Preheat oven to 400 degrees.

Melt butter in a saucepan. Add flour, blend, and cook over low heat 2 to 3 minutes. Add milk and cook, stirring, until sauce thickens and is smooth. Cook over low heat 3 to 4 minutes more. Stir in grated cheese. Remove saucepan from heat and add egg yolks, one at a time, beating well after each addition. Add asparagus and seasonings.

In the bowl of an electric mixer, beat egg whites with a dash of salt and the cream of tartar. Beat until whites are stiff but not dry. *Do not overbeat.* Stir one-fourth of the beaten whites into the base to lighten. Fold in remaining whites using a large rubber spatula. Turn bowl with other hand and use your spatula to gently incorporate the whites. Pour mixture into prepared dish and bake 25 to 30 minutes, until soufflé has sufficiently puffed and is golden brown. Serve at once.

Thai Omelet

My husband, Carl, and I enjoyed this simple but delicious omelet on the terrace of the legendary Oriental Hotel in Bangkok. As we savored our omelet bite by bite, we were able to watch the colorful river traffic pass by.

Yield: Two small (8-inch) omelets

Vegetable oil
2 tablespoons finely chopped shallots
2 tablespoons finely chopped pork meat
3 eggs, lightly beaten
1 tablespoon Thai fish sauce *(nam pla)*
1 tablespoon snipped chives or scallion tops (green part)
Salt and freshly ground pepper to taste

Heat 1 teaspoon oil in nonstick frying pan and sauté shallots and pork until meat loses color (1 to 2 minutes). Cool slightly, then combine with eggs, fish sauce, chives or scallions, and salt and pepper, and mix well. Pour half the mixture into a hot nonstick frying pan that has been brushed with vegetable oil and cook 1 minute. Turn the omelet into a second heated and oiled nonstick skillet (or simply turn over) and cook 1 to 2 minutes. Serve with the following sauce.

To make sauce:

---

4 tablespoons fish sauce
1 small red or green fresh chile pepper, seeded and cut into tiny pieces

Combine ingredients and mix well.

New Joe's Special

New Joe's Special originated at New Joe's Restaurant, a landmark restaurant in San Francisco. It was known for late-night dining and specialized in burgers, pastas ("Always use your fork, never use a tablespoon as a helper"), and the famous New Joe's Special, a unique and satisfying comfort food. Carl and I began our married life in San Francisco, and early on went to New Joe's. Throughout our stay we returned many times, always ordering New Joe's Special.

Yield: 6–8 servings

4 tablespoons olive oil
4 tablespoons unsalted butter
1 bunch scallions, finely chopped
1½ pounds ground beef (I prefer freshly ground chuck)
1 package (12 ounces) fresh baby spinach, washed and spun dry
8 eggs, lightly beaten
½ cup freshly grated Parmesan cheese
Salt and freshly ground pepper

Heat oil and butter in a skillet, add chopped scallions, and cook until soft but not brown. Add meat, break up with a fork, and cook until juices in the bottom of the pan are dry. Add spinach, mix well, and cook until wilted. Add eggs, cheese, salt, and pepper and mix with a spatula, being careful not to let eggs stick on the bottom of the pan. Cook until eggs are set, about 3 to 4 minutes.

SALADS

CLASSIC SALAD NIÇOISE
40

COBB SALAD
41

FATTOUSH
42

INSALATA VERDE
44

PARK BISTRO WARM GOAT CHEESE
ON POTATO SALAD
45

SUMMER ORZO SALAD
46

WINTER SALAD WITH BELGIAN ENDIVE,
HARICOTS VERTS, AND TOASTED HAZELNUTS
48

Classic Salad Niçoise

*B*efore I spent time in Cannes on the French Riviera, I made Salad Niçoise, but it never tasted as good as it did when I prepared the salad in France. I think it was the authentic ingredients: French haricots verts, light (not pure white) canned tuna packed in olive oil, authentic Niçoise olives and anchovies, and fine French olive oil and vinegar. It is possible to do a pretty good job at home if you are careful to buy the best quality, fresh ingredients.

Yield: 6–8 servings

2 small or 1 large head romaine or leaf lettuce, or a combination,
    broken into bite-size pieces
½ cup chopped sweet or red onion
1 jar (11 ounces) Italian solid tuna packed in olive oil, flaked
1½ cups blanched haricots verts, or other fresh green beans
1 green or red bell pepper, cut into rings
⅓ cup Niçoise olives, or other black olives of your choice
3 hard-boiled eggs, quartered
3 tomatoes, quartered
1 can flat anchovies (reserve 4 for dressing)
¼ cup finely chopped herbs (tarragon, chervil, parsley, and basil preferred)

Place lettuce in bowl. Add onions, tuna, green beans, pepper rings, and black olives. Arrange quartered eggs, tomatoes, and anchovies over top and sprinkle with herb mixture. Cover lightly with foil or wax paper and refrigerate until serving time.

Vinaigrette Niçoise

4 anchovies
1 hard-boiled egg
2 tablespoons mixed herbs (parsley, tarragon, and chervil)
Freshly ground pepper
1 tablespoon Dijon mustard
3 tablespoons white wine vinegar
¾ cup extra-virgin olive oil

With a mortar and pestle, or blending fork, mash anchovies, egg, and herbs into a paste. Add pepper, mustard, wine vinegar, and olive oil. Adjust seasonings, adding salt if necessary.

COBB SALAD

I first tasted Cobb Salad in Palm Springs, and it was perfect—artfully created and beautifully served. I have little patience for fake Cobb Salads, and the recipe below is a California original. Cobb Salad is a chopped salad, and all ingredients should be diced, cubed, or cut into julienne.

Yield: 6 servings

2 medium heads hearts of romaine
1 large chicken breast, cooked (preferably grilled)
¼ pound bacon (about 6–8 strips), fried crisp and crumbled
½ cup Danish Blue or other blue cheese, coarsely grated
2–3 hard-boiled eggs, coarsely grated
1 avocado
Lemon juice
1 bunch scallions, green tops snipped, white parts sliced into small circles
2–3 tomatoes, peeled, seeded, and diced

Cut 2 medium heads of romaine hearts crosswise into small pieces and line the bottom of a large salad bowl with a bed of greens. Remove the skin and bones from the chicken breast and cut meat into julienne strips. Add bacon and cheese. Add hard-boiled eggs. Dice avocado and brush with lemon juice to prevent discoloring.

Arrange the ingredients in stripes over the greens: chicken, bacon, cheese, eggs (I like to separate white and yellow), avocado, scallions, and tomatoes. Drizzle with vinaigrette dressing.

continued

Vinaigrette dressing

2 tablespoons red wine vinegar
½ teaspoon salt
Freshly ground pepper to taste
½ cup olive oil

Whisk ingredients in a small bowl and pour over salad. Serve immediately.

Fattoush

Fattoush is one of my favorite salads, and it is best made with tomatoes and cucumbers in season. The feta cheese, toasted pita bread, and fresh mint add a true Middle Eastern dimension. This salad never fails to please and may be used as a first or main course, depending on the rest of your menu.

Yield: 6 servings

¼ cup olive oil
2–3 medium-sized cloves of garlic, pressed or minced
2 7-inch pita breads
1 large or 2 medium heads romaine lettuce, torn into bite-size pieces
½ cup diced mild onion
1 medium-sized cucumber, peeled, seeded, and sliced
3 medium tomatoes, cut into wedges
12 Kalamata olives
1 cup crumbled feta cheese
½ cup finely chopped parsley
¼ cup chopped fresh mint, or 1 tablespoon dried
1 teaspoon zatar (blend of marjoram, thyme, toasted sesame seeds, and ground sumac), optional
Salt and freshly ground pepper

Preheat oven to 375 degrees.

Mix olive oil and minced garlic. Split pita breads into rounds and brush the insides with garlic oil. Place on baking sheet and bake until crisp, about 5 minutes. Cool, and then break into bite-sized pieces.

Put lettuce into a salad bowl. Add vegetables and cheese. Sprinkle with parsley, mint, and optional zatar. Add 5 to 6 tablespoons of dressing and toss greens to coat well. Add pieces of pita and more dressing, if desired, season, and toss again.

DRESSING

2 tablespoons lemon juice
1 clove garlic, minced or pressed
½ teaspoon zatar (optional)
2 tablespoons fresh mint, or 1 teaspoon dried
½ cup extra-virgin olive oil
Salt and pepper to taste

Combine all ingredients in a small bowl and whisk until blended.

INSALATA VERDE

*I*nsalata Verde is my idea of a delicious Italian salad. I love the addition of fennel for taste and texture, and the radishes and cauliflower for color and crunch. The Gorgonzola cheese adds smoothness and, combined with the grated hard-boiled egg, provides an interesting texture and touch of color.

Yield: 4–6 servings

1 large or 2 small heads romaine lettuce
1 small fennel bulb, shaved or thinly sliced
6 radishes, sliced thin
1 cup cauliflower florets
6–8 Kalamata olives
1 cup crumbled or coarsely grated Gorgonzola cheese
1 hard-boiled egg, coarsely grated
Finely chopped fresh parsley

Wash and dry salad greens. Tear into pieces and place in a bowl. Add the fennel, radishes, cauliflower florets, and Kalamata olives. Combine Gorgonzola, grated egg, and parsley and sprinkle over greens, then toss the salad with the following dressing.

DRESSING

3 anchovies, chopped and mashed (or anchovy paste equivalent)
1 teaspoon Dijon mustard
Freshly ground pepper
2 tablespoons red wine vinegar
½ cup extra-virgin olive oil
Salt to taste

Combine mashed anchovies and mustard. Add pepper and wine vinegar and mix well. Whisk in olive oil. Add salt to taste and toss with greens.

Park Bistro Warm Goat Cheese on Potato Salad

*P*ark Bistro Warm Goat Cheese on Potato Salad makes an excellent first course for a dinner party. The recipe originated many years ago at the Park Bistro restaurant in New York. The young French chef came from Restaurant Jacques Chibois in Cannes.

Yield: 8 servings

1½ pounds new potatoes
3 shallots, finely chopped
¼ cup balsamic vinegar
Salt and freshly ground pepper
¾ cup extra-virgin olive oil
⅓ cup chopped fresh herbs (basil, flat-leaf parsley, chives, thyme, tarragon, etc.)
Fresh goat cheese, crumbled or grated for topping (1–1½ cups)
Cream-egg mixture (¼ cup heavy cream, mixed with 1 egg yolk)
6 cups mixed greens (baby lettuces, romaine, Bibb, radicchio, watercress)

Cover potatoes with salted water, bring to a boil, cover, and cook at a steady boil until barely tender (for medium potatoes about 15 minutes). When cool, peel and slice ¼ to ½ inch thick.

Make a vinaigrette by combining shallots, vinegar, salt, pepper, and olive oil. Use about one-half of the dressing to moisten potatoes. Season with salt and pepper and toss with chopped herbs. Reserve remaining dressing for greens.

Preheat oven to 300 degrees.

On a baking sheet, using metal rings (3 to 4 inches in diameter), mold potato salad into rounds (may be done free-form or with improvised tinfoil rings). Top with goat cheese and warm in oven 5 minutes. Brush with cream-egg mixture and glaze under broiler.

Place salad greens in bowl and toss lightly with dressing. Divide among plates and place potato rounds on top of or adjacent to greens. Drizzle with any remaining dressing and garnish with any remaining herbs.

Summer Orzo Salad

To make Roasted Plum Tomatoes:

Plum tomatoes (approximately 2–3 pounds)
Good-quality olive oil
Salt and freshly ground pepper

Preheat oven to 275 degrees. Line a baking sheet with a silicone baking mat or parchment paper.

Cut tomatoes in half. Place tomato halves on lined baking sheet, first cutting a small slice from bottom of each tomato half. Brush tomato halves with olive oil and season with salt and freshly ground pepper. Roast tomatoes about 3 hours, or until lightly browned on top. When cool enough to handle, remove skin. Store well covered in the refrigerator.

Roasted garlic:

1 whole head garlic
Extra-virgin olive oil
Salt and freshly ground pepper
Fresh or dried thyme

Preheat oven to 350 degrees.

Cut off ½ inch from top of garlic head. Brush with olive oil; season with salt, freshly ground pepper, and thyme. Bake approximately 1 hour in a garlic baker or wrapped in foil.

2 cups orzo

5–6 tablespoons extra-virgin olive oil, divided

Salt and freshly ground pepper

Basil, cut in chiffonade

2 cups chopped roasted plum tomatoes

1 head roasted garlic

¼ cup water

Cook orzo in a pot of boiling salted water 15 minutes, or until tender. Drain and run briefly under cold water. Drain again. Combine orzo and 3 to 4 tablespoons of the extra-virgin olive oil in a bowl. Season with salt and freshly ground pepper, add basil to taste—enough to provide flavor and color—and combine well.

Heat remaining 2 tablespoons of olive oil in a frying pan. Add tomatoes and cook 2 minutes. Squeeze garlic pulp out of skins into tomatoes and mix well. Add ¼ cup water, bring to a boil, and simmer, covered, 5 to 10 minutes.

Toss tomato sauce with orzo, blending well. Adjust seasoning and serve at room temperature.

Summer Orzo Salad may be prepared ahead and refrigerated, but should be served at room temperature.

WINTER SALAD WITH BELGIAN ENDIVE, HARICOTS VERTS, AND TOASTED HAZELNUTS

*H*ere is a lovely salad designed for entertaining, but one your family should certainly enjoy. I have expanded on Roger Verge's Haricots Verts and Hazelnuts by adding some lovely greens, some Belgian endive for texture, and roasted red pepper for color. The salad makes an elegant presentation.

Yield: 6–8 servings

4–5 small heads of Bibb lettuce, in bite-size pieces
4 heads Belgian endive, in bite-size pieces
½ pound haricots verts (small, tender green beans), tailed
1 large roasted red bell pepper, cut into julienne
Mâche or watercress
Snipped fresh chives
½ cup blanched and toasted hazelnuts, coarsely chopped

Place Bibb lettuce and Belgian endive pieces in a large salad bowl.

Blanch green beans in a 4-quart pot of boiling salted water for 2 minutes, or until almost tender but still firm to the bite. Drain and plunge into a bowl of ice water for 4 to 5 minutes, drain, and dry on paper toweling or a kitchen towel.

Scatter beans on top of greens and add julienne roasted red pepper. Top with about 2 cups mâche or watercress leaves. Garnish with chives and scatter hazelnuts over top. If desired, hazelnuts may be warmed in a toaster or regular oven. Toss with the following dressing and serve.

LEMON VINAIGRETTE

1 tablespoon minced shallots
1 teaspoon Dijon mustard
Salt and freshly ground pepper to taste
1–2 teaspoons grated lemon rind
1 tablespoon lemon juice
½ teaspoon balsamic vinegar
2 tablespoons walnut oil
2 tablespoons extra-virgin olive oil
4 tablespoons grapeseed or light vegetable oil
Touch of heavy cream (optional)

Combine shallots, mustard, salt, freshly ground pepper, and lemon rind in a small bowl. Add lemon juice and vinegar. Whisk in oils, blending well. If desired, dressing may be finished with a splash of heavy cream.

Between the lines: To remove the skin from red, orange, or yellow bell peppers, place on a baking sheet under a preheated broiler. Broil peppers, turning as skin darkens. When lightly charred, remove and place in a paper or plastic bag to cool for easy removal of skin.

SOUPS AND STEWS

CHILLED CUCUMBER BISQUE
52

GAZPACHO WITH GRILLED SHRIMP
53

SAFFRON POTATO BISQUE
54

CALDO VERDE
55

LIMA BEAN SOUP
56

ONION SOUP MARSEILLE
57

SOUPE AU PISTOU
58

CELERY AND CELERY ROOT BISQUE
59

TUSCAN BEAN SOUP
60

CHOUCROUTE GARNIE AU CHAMPAGNE
62

FRENCH BEEF RAGOUT
63

HUNGARIAN GOULASH
64

JANE'S RED CHILI
65

Chilled Cucumber Bisque

I first tasted Chilled Cucumber Bisque when I was newly married. My husband and I were in Los Angeles for a visit in 1955 and Scandia was famous for Danish dishes. I don't remember what else we ordered, but the Chilled Cucumber Bisque has remained a favorite.

Yield: 8 generous or 10 small servings

2 "English" hothouse cucumbers, or 4 medium regular cucumbers
2 tablespoons unsalted butter
1 cup sliced leeks (white part only)
1 bay leaf
1 rounded tablespoon flour
3 cups chicken stock
1 teaspoon salt
1 cup heavy cream, or to taste
Juice of ½ lemon
⅓ cup chopped or finely cut mixed fresh herbs (dill, chives, basil, or parsley)
Salt and freshly ground pepper to taste

Peel cucumbers, cut in half lengthwise, and remove seeds with the tip of a teaspoon. Cut enough cucumbers into small dice to yield between 2½ and 3 cups. Reserve remaining cucumber for later.

Melt butter in a saucepan and cook cucumbers with leeks and bay leaf, covered, over low heat for 15 minutes. Do not brown. A buttered round of wax paper placed directly on top of vegetables avoids browning.

Add flour, blend, pour in chicken stock, add salt, and mix well. Bring to a boil, cover, lower heat to a simmer, and cook 30 minutes. Remove bay leaf, cool, then pour into food processor or blender and puree until smooth.

Coarsely grate remaining cucumber and salt lightly. Drain a few minutes to remove excess water and add to soup, along with heavy cream and lemon juice. Stir in herbs, correct seasoning, and chill several hours or overnight.

Gazpacho with Grilled Shrimp

*G*azpacho with Grilled Shrimp is a flavorful tomato-based soup that incorporates some of the ingredients found in traditional Spanish gazpacho. By adding grilled shrimp at the last minute to the cold soup, it is possible to create an elegant and different gazpacho.

Yield: 6–8 servings

---

3 pounds very ripe tomatoes, peeled, seeded, and coarsely chopped
½ large red bell pepper, stemmed, peeled, seeded, and coarsely chopped
½ large "English" hothouse cucumber, peeled, seeded, and coarsely chopped
1 teaspoon finely chopped garlic
4 tablespoons extra-virgin olive oil
¼ cup sherry wine vinegar, or to taste
1 tablespoon tomato paste
Salt and freshly ground pepper to taste
1 pound shrimp, shelled and deveined (recommended size 21 and under to the pound)
Extra-virgin olive oil
Salt and freshly ground pepper

Puree vegetables in a food processor with the garlic, oil, vinegar, tomato paste, salt, and pepper. Add 1 cup of cold water, or more if you prefer thinner soup, and refrigerate several hours or overnight, until well chilled.

Preheat a stovetop grill. Brush shrimp with olive oil, season with salt and freshly ground pepper, and grill, turning once, until shrimp are no longer translucent and are cooked through, about 3 to 4 minutes.

Ladle soup into shallow bowls, add 2 shrimp to each bowl, and serve.

Between the lines: The soup base may be made a few days ahead, but I would not recommend freezing. Many years ago I discovered the small cast-iron stovetop grill and I use it often. The grill does an amazing job grilling vegetables, small pieces of meat or chicken, and bread. The grill marks are attractive.

Saffron Potato Bisque

Here is a slightly different twist on classic vichyssoise. Spanish saffron adds a unique flavor and color, and the toasted almonds provide a contrast to the velvety smooth soup.

Yield: 12 servings

4 cups peeled, diced raw potatoes (3–4 medium Idaho or Yukon Gold)
5 cloves garlic, mashed
1 leek, thinly sliced (white part only)
Salt and freshly ground pepper
A generous pinch of saffron (powder or threads)
4 cups chicken stock
1½ cups milk
Additional chicken stock to thin chilled soup, if necessary (¾–1 cup)
1 cup heavy cream, or to taste
Pinch of cayenne pepper
⅓ cup blanched, slivered almonds, lightly toasted
Snipped fresh chives

Combine potatoes, garlic, leek, salt, pepper, saffron, and chicken stock in a heavy saucepan. Bring to a boil, lower heat, and simmer, partially covered, until potatoes are tender, about 20 minutes. Stir in milk and bring to a boil. Remove from heat, pass mixture through a food mill (fine disk) or fine strainer, and chill overnight.

After soup has chilled thin with enough cold chicken stock to make a smooth texture. Add cream to taste. Adjust seasonings and chill one more hour before serving.

Sprinkle with toasted almonds and chives.

Between the lines: Saffron is a very expensive spice from Spain. I prefer powdered saffron, but in the United States, it is very hard to find. There are no substitutes for saffron. Buy the best quality available from reliable sources. A little saffron goes a long way; use sparingly.

CALDO VERDE

Caldo Verde is a substantial and hearty vegetable soup of peasant origin that is satisfying and delicious and healthy, too. The soup is a perfect choice for vegetarian friends. Caldo Verde originated in Portugal. It calls for common, everyday ingredients and requires no stock, only water and bouillon cubes if desired.

Yield: 12 servings

1 pound Great Northern or other dried white beans, soaked in water overnight
1 bunch kale (6–7 cups)
4 cups turnip greens
½ cup olive oil
3 medium yellow onions, finely chopped (about 2 cups)
½ pound potatoes, peeled and coarsely grated
Salt and freshly ground pepper to taste
3 quarts water flavored with 2–3 bouillon cubes

Drain beans. Remove large ribs from kale and slice into thin strips. Repeat with turnip greens.

Heat olive oil in a large soup pot. Add onions and sauté to soften, but do not brown. Add greens and cook until wilted. Add potatoes and beans, and season with salt and pepper. Add water and bouillon cubes, mix well, and bring to a boil. Lower heat, cover pot, and cook at a simmer for 1½ hours.

Using a food mill, puree as many cups of the soup back into the pot as necessary to reach desired thickness. Leave some whole beans and greens for texture. If soup is too thin, reduce heat, being careful not to burn the bottom, for additional thickening. Adjust seasonings and serve.

LIMA BEAN SOUP

*T*his recipe originated at the Gazebo delicatessen in Shadyside. Though Clarence, who made the soup, and the delicatessen are no more, the soup lives on in my house. Loved by many and missed by all, the Gazebo made delicious homemade soups and wonderful Reuben sandwiches.

Yield: 12 servings

2 pounds large dry lima beans
4 tablespoons good-quality olive oil
1 cup chopped onions
1 cup chopped celery
1 cup chopped carrots
3 quarts homemade or good-quality canned chicken stock
1 28-ounce can whole tomatoes, chopped
1 small bunch fresh dill
Salt and freshly ground pepper to taste

Soak beans overnight. Drain. Heat olive oil in a large pot, add onions, celery, and carrots, and cook over low heat 10 minutes, stirring occasionally. Stir in lima beans and cook an additional few minutes. Add chicken stock and tomatoes. Bring to a boil, lower heat, and simmer, covered, about 2 hours. Add dill, cook long enough to wilt, and adjust seasonings. Puree about one-quarter of the mixture through a food mill back into the pot to thicken the soup and give it body and texture.

Onion Soup Marseille

*O*nion Soup Marseille bears little resemblance to classic French Onion Soup or Soupe de Poisson from Marseille. I used this recipe in my first cooking classes. Ingredients are few and readily available. The soup is easy to do, and best of all, it is delicious!

Yield: 8 servings

---

2 large sweet onions (about 1½ pounds)
4 tablespoons good-quality olive oil
¼ teaspoon sugar
2 cloves garlic, minced
2 tablespoons flour
1 cup dry white wine
1 cup canned Italian plum tomatoes, with juices
4 cups chicken or fish stock
½–1 cup heavy cream
2–3 tablespoons Pernod or other unsweetened anise-flavored liqueur

---

Cut onions in half. Cut each half into thin slices. You should have about 6 cups. In a heavy saucepan, heat olive oil, add onions, and cook over medium-low heat, until onions are golden, stirring occasionally. To hasten browning, sprinkle with ¼ teaspoon sugar and cook, covered, for 10 to 15 minutes. Stir in garlic and cook an additional 2 minutes.

Sprinkle with flour and stir to blend. Cook 1 to 2 minutes, and then add wine, tomatoes, and stock. Bring to a boil, lower heat, cover, and cook at a simmer for 30 minutes.

Add cream and just bring to a boil. Add Pernod and cook a few additional minutes.

Between the lines: The French aperitif Pernod adds a licorice-like flavor that makes this soup rather distinctive. You may achieve a similar result by lightly toasting anise seeds and pulverizing fine before adding to the soup.

Soupe au Pistou

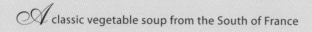

*classic vegetable soup from the South of France

Yield: 12 servings

½ pound dried white beans
4 ounces sliced salt pork (optional)
1½ cups peeled and chopped carrots
1 stalk celery, diced
3 leeks, white part only, thinly sliced
4 medium potatoes, peeled and diced
5 tomatoes, peeled and chopped
2 cups green beans, diced
2 cups zucchini, diced
½ cup small-cut dried soup pasta
Salt and pepper to taste

Cover dried beans with cold water and soak overnight. Drain and place in a large pot with 4 quarts water and optional salt pork. Bring to a boil, lower heat, and simmer, covered, 30 minutes.

Add carrots, celery, leeks, potatoes, and tomatoes and simmer soup another 30 minutes. Add green beans, zucchini, and pasta and cook 20 minutes longer. Remove salt pork and season soup. If desired, pass a few cups of soup through the food mill for a thicker texture. Right before serving, add pistou to taste and pass freshly grated Parmesan cheese.

Pistou

---

2 bunches fresh basil
8–10 cloves garlic, chopped or crushed
8–12 tablespoons olive oil
Salt and freshly ground pepper to taste
Freshly grated Parmesan cheese

Combine in food processor and blend until smooth.

Celery and Celery Root Bisque

This soup makes an elegant first course to any formal meal. The flavor is sublime.

Yield: 8–10 servings

---

4 tablespoons (½ stick) unsalted butter
1 medium onion, coarsely chopped
1 leek (white part only), sliced
3 stalks of celery, stringed and sliced
1 bay leaf
2 medium Idaho potatoes, peeled and cut into large dice
1 medium to large celery root, peeled and cut into large dice
Salt and freshly ground pepper (preferably white) to taste
8 cups chicken stock
½ cinnamon stick
½–1 cup heavy cream
Celery leaves or thinly sliced black truffle for garnish

In a 4-quart saucepan, melt butter over low heat. Add onion, leek, and celery and cook until vegetables are soft, about 10 minutes. Add bay leaf, potatoes, and celery root and cook another 5 minutes. Season with salt and freshly ground pepper.

Add stock and bring to a boil over medium heat. Reduce heat to low, add cinnamon stick, and simmer, covered, 30 minutes, or until celery root is soft. Remove cinnamon stick and puree soup in small batches in a food processor. Strain, pressing hard on the solids. Pour the strained soup into a clean saucepan, add cream to taste, adjust seasonings, and heat soup until hot.

Serve in individual bowls and garnish with the celery leaves or a thin slices of black truffle.

TUSCAN BEAN SOUP

On a trip to Italy with a group of food and wine enthusiasts, we stopped at Fattoria dei Barbi outside of Montalcino for a wine tasting and lunch. The winery prepared authentic Tuscan Bean Soup. The soup was delicious and made even more so by the last-minute addition of thinly sliced onion, a slice of toasted Tuscan bread, and a drizzle of locally made olive oil to each serving. With a glass of red wine from the winery, this was a meal to remember.

Yield: 10 servings

---

2 cups dried cannellini beans, soaked in cold water to cover overnight
2 cloves garlic, smashed
1 large rib celery, cut in half
Handful of parsley stems
Salt
½ cup olive oil
3 medium onions, finely chopped
3 carrots, peeled and cut into small dice
3 ribs celery, stringed and cut into small dice
Salt and freshly ground pepper
3 ripe Italian plum tomatoes (fresh or canned), peeled, seeded, and diced
⅓ cup tomato puree, or 1–2 tablespoons tomato paste
1–2 cups chicken stock
3 leaves Swiss chard or spinach
3 leaves purple cabbage (optional)
4 cups thinly sliced Savoy cabbage
8–10 slices day-old Italian bread, toasted
1 large onion, cut into thin rings
Extra-virgin olive oil

To cook beans: Drain beans and discard discolored ones. Return beans to pot and cover with cold water (8 to 10 cups). Add the smashed garlic, celery rib, and parsley stems. Bring the beans to a boil over high heat. Turn down to a simmer, partially cover, and cook until beans are tender—about 1 to 1½ hours—adding salt the last half hour.

While beans are cooking, heat olive oil in a large pot and sauté onions, carrots, and diced celery until translucent. Season with salt and freshly ground pepper. Mix in diced tomatoes and cook a few minutes, then blend in tomato puree. Add cooked beans, with their cooking liquid, to the vegetables. Add chicken stock.

Cut the chard and the purple cabbage into strips. Add to the soup with Savoy cabbage. Cook, covered, for 1 hour over medium heat. Pass approximately two-thirds of the soup through a food mill (second choice: food processor) back into pot. Adjust seasoning and simmer 15 to 20 minutes longer.

For each serving, place a slice of bread and some onion rings in individual bowls. Add soup and pass extra-virgin olive oil.

Between the lines: Cannellini beans are Italian white beans that are similar to Great Northern beans, which may be used instead.

Choucroute Garnie au Champagne

Yield: 10–12 servings

---

1 pound salt pork, thinly sliced
2 large onions, sliced
4 cloves garlic, coarsely chopped
4 pounds uncooked sauerkraut, well washed*
1 large piece German speck, or additional salt pork (½–¾ pound)
Freshly ground pepper
1 teaspoon juniper berries
Champagne or dry white wine
Vegetable oil
1 boned loin of pork (about 2½–3 pounds)
1 large saucisson d'ail or other garlic sausage
6–10 small sausages (bockwurst, bratwurst, knockwurst, frankfurters)
Boiled potatoes

Line a deep casserole or roasting pan with the thinly sliced salt pork; add half the sliced onions and chopped garlic. Place a thick layer of well-washed sauerkraut on top, with the large piece of speck or salt pork. Grind plenty of pepper over the top, sprinkle with juniper berries, and add remaining onions and garlic. Cover with remaining sauerkraut and add just enough champagne or dry white wine to barely cover the sauerkraut. Cover and cook in a 300-degree oven for 4 to 6 hours.

In a skillet, heat a small amount of vegetable oil. Brown pork loin and sausages on all sides. Two hours before serving, add pork loin to casserole, and 30 minutes before completion, add sausages.

Heap the sauerkraut in the middle of a platter and arrange slices of meat and sausages attractively on top. Traditionally, an unopened half-bottle of champagne, wires removed, is placed in the center of the hot sauerkraut just before presentation. As the bottle warms, the cork is forced out and the champagne gushes forth. I suggest pouring champagne over the choucroute at the table right before serving. Serve with boiled potatoes.

*To prepare sauerkraut properly for braising, drain and soak in a large bowl of cold water for 30 minutes, changing the water three times. Taste the sauerkraut, and when the briny flavor is gone, drain and remove as much water as possible by squeezing. Fluff the strands for cooking.

French Beef Ragout

---

4 pounds boneless chuck roast, trimmed and cut into 1–1½-inch cubes
   (2½–3 pounds after trimming)
Salt and freshly ground pepper
1 tablespoon thyme, or 1 teaspoon dried
3 tablespoons olive oil
1 tablespoon minced garlic
¼ cup finely chopped parsley
½ cup *each* finely chopped onion, carrot, and celery
½ pound salt pork, cut into ¼-inch strips and blanched in boiling water
5 tablespoons flour
3 cups red wine
2 cups chicken stock
2 tablespoons tomato paste
1 bay leaf
2 teaspoons currant jelly
¾–1 pound pearl onions, blanched
1 pound mushrooms, left whole if small, quartered if large
3–4 tablespoons butter

Season meat with salt and pepper and place in a large bowl or dish. Add thyme, olive oil, garlic, parsley, onion, carrot, and celery. Mix well, cover, and refrigerate a few hours or overnight.

In a Dutch oven or large pot, render salt pork until crisp. Remove and drain on paper toweling. Brown the meat cubes in rendered fat over high heat, stirring and turning the pieces often, about 10 minutes. Do not crowd the pan; do the browning in batches. With the last batch, scrape the bowl, adding marinated vegetables.

Return meat to pot, sprinkle with flour, stir to combine, and cook 2 minutes. Add wine, chicken stock, tomato paste, bay leaf, and currant jelly. Bring to a boil, lower heat, cover, and simmer 1 hour.

After 1 hour, sauté onions and mushrooms in a large frying pan in melted butter. Cook 5 minutes, add to meat, and simmer an additional half hour.

Hungarian Goulash

Yield: 8 servings

---

4 tablespoons butter
4 tablespoons vegetable oil
4 cups sliced onions (about 1 pound)
3 pounds boneless veal, cut into well-trimmed cubes
Salt and freshly ground pepper
1–2 tablespoons finely chopped garlic
4 tablespoons flour
4 tablespoons Hungarian paprika
3 cups chicken stock
2 tablespoons tomato paste

Gremolata (Seasoning Paste)

½ teaspoon salt
1 tablespoon chopped fresh marjoram, or 1 teaspoon dried
2 teaspoons caraway seeds, crushed
1 lemon rind, grated
2 cloves garlic, minced
¼ cup finely chopped parsley

In a Dutch oven or similar cooking pot, heat half the butter and oil and slowly cook the onions, stirring often, until soft but not brown.

Heat remaining butter and oil in a large frying pan. Season meat with salt and freshly ground pepper and, over medium-high heat, sauté meat, being sure not to crowd the pan, until cubes are nicely browned. Add meat to onions with garlic and cook 2 minutes. Combine flour and paprika and sprinkle over meat and onions. Cook about 3 minutes, blending well.

Deglaze frying pan in which meat has been cooked with 1 cup of chicken stock. Add to Dutch oven with remaining 2 cups of chicken stock and tomato paste, mixing well. Bring pot to boil, cover, and cook on top of the stove at a gentle simmer for about 1 hour.

Make a paste of the salt, marjoram, caraway seeds, chopped lemon rind, garlic, and parsley and add to goulash right before serving. Serve goulash with spaetzle or egg noodles.

Jane's Red Chili

Yield: 8–10 servings

---

5 pounds lean chuck roast, trimmed of fat and cut into 1-inch cubes
Salt and freshly ground pepper
½ cup olive oil
1 tablespoon toasted cumin seeds
1 tablespoon dried oregano
10 cloves garlic, minced
½ cup flour
½ cup chili powder*
4 cups homemade or canned chicken or beef broth

Season meat cubes with salt and pepper. Heat olive oil in a large pot or kettle and add the cubed meat. Cook, turning occasionally, until meat loses red color. Pulverize cumin seeds and oregano by hand or in a small grinder and add to meat with minced garlic, mixing well. Combine flour and chili powder and sift or strain over meat, stirring to combine. Add broth, bring mixture to a boil, lower heat, and simmer, partly covered, for approximately 4 to 5 hours, until meat is very tender and sauce has reduced and thickened.

Serve with pinto beans, rice, or mashed potatoes and a selection of garnishes—salsa, sour cream, guacamole, grated cheddar cheese, shredded lettuce, chopped onions, cilantro, and flour tortillas.

*I used chili claro from Reyna's Foods in the Strip District.

Pinto Beans

---

1 pound dried pinto beans
1 large onion, chopped
½ pound salt pork
Salt and pepper to taste

Soak beans in water to cover 1 hour, then drain. Cover again with water to 2 inches above the beans, and add onion and salt pork. Bring to a boil, cover, lower heat, and simmer until beans are tender, about 2 hours. Season to taste.

PASTA

FIDELINI AND OVEN-ROASTED TOMATOES,
ROASTED GARLIC, AND CLAMS
68

LINGUINE WITH WHITE CLAM SAUCE
70

ORECCHIETTE PASTA WITH
PANCETTA, CABBAGE, AND ITALIAN CHEESE
71

PASTA MAFALDA
72

SPAGHETTI ALL'ORTOLANA
73

FIDELINI AND OVEN-ROASTED TOMATOES, ROASTED GARLIC, AND CLAMS

*F*idelini is a very thin long pasta similar to capellini or angel hair.

Yield: 8 small servings

OVEN-ROASTED TOMATOES

Ripe but not soft plum tomatoes (15 or 20)
Extra-virgin olive oil
Salt and freshly ground pepper

Preheat oven to 250 degrees. Line a baking sheet with parchment paper or a silicone baking mat. Cut tomatoes in half horizontally. Remove stem from one half and cut a thin slice off the bottom of the other half. Place tomato halves on baking sheet. Brush tomatoes with olive oil and season with salt and pepper. Place in oven and roast 2 to 3 hours, until tomato skin shrinks and tomatoes are cooked but still hold their shape. Slip off skins and use in recipe or freeze.

ROASTED GARLIC

Whole heads of garlic
Olive oil
Salt and freshly ground pepper
Few sprigs fresh thyme

Preheat oven to 350 degrees. Cut a ½-inch slice horizontally, removing the top of each head of garlic. Place in a garlic baker. Sprinkle with olive oil, and season with salt and pepper and sprigs of thyme. Cover and roast until soft, about 45 to 60 minutes. (If you do not have a garlic baker, wrap prepared garlic in foil and bake.)

To prepare clams:

2 dozen littleneck clams
1 cup water
1 cup wine
4 cloves garlic, crushed
1 small onion, sliced
4 or 5 black peppercorns
Bouquet garni (sprig parsley, thyme, and bay leaf)

Soak clams in a pot of cold water for 10 to 15 minutes. Using a brush or scouring pad, scrub clams and rinse well. Place clams in a pot, and cover with water and wine. Add garlic, onion, peppercorns, and bouquet garni. Bring to a boil, cover, and steam until clams open. Remove clams to a side dish and pass liquid through a strainer lined with cheesecloth to remove any sand. Reserve clams, leaving some clams in shell for garnish, and adding the rest to cooking liquid.

Sauce for Fidelini

¼ cup extra-virgin olive oil
15 oven-roasted tomatoes, coarsely chopped
1–2 heads roasted garlic, cloves pressed into paste
Reserved clam broth and clams
½ cup chopped flat-leaf parsley

Heat olive oil in a 12-inch frying pan. Add tomatoes and garlic and sauté a few minutes, stirring frequently. Add reserved clam broth with clams and blend well. Simmer a few minutes to blend flavors, add clams and parsley, and adjust seasonings.

To serve:

¾ pound fidelini pasta

Bring a large pot of salted water to a boil. Add fidelini and cook al dente. Drain but do not rinse. Toss fidelini with sauce. Serve in warm bowls and garnish with reserved clams in the shell.

Linguine with White Clam Sauce

Yield: 4 main-course servings

---

2 dozen littleneck clams
1 cup water
1 cup wine
4 cloves garlic, crushed
2 shallots, sliced
1 jalapeño pepper, seeded and cut into small dice
Bouquet garni (sprig parsley, thyme, and bay leaf)

Place clams in a pot, and cover with water and wine. Add garlic, shallots, jalapeño pepper, and bouquet garni. Bring to a boil, cover, and steam until clams open. Remove clams to a side dish and pass liquid through a strainer lined with cheesecloth to remove any sand. Reserve clams and cooking liquid.

---

3 tablespoons olive oil
3 tablespoons finely chopped shallots
1 tablespoon minced garlic
1 jalapeño pepper, seeded and cut into small dice
1 can (7¾ ounces) chopped clams
Reserved cooking liquid
1 tablespoon dried oregano
½ cup chopped flat-leaf parsley, divided
½ cup heavy cream
Cornstarch slurry (1 tablespoon cornstarch dissolved in 3 tablespoons cold water)
Salt and freshly ground pepper to taste
¾ pound linguine

Heat oil in a saucepan. Add shallots, garlic, and jalapeño pepper and sauté until transparent and soft but not brown. Add chopped canned clams with their liquid, oregano, ¼ cup of the parsley, and reserved cooking liquid. Bring to a boil, cover, and simmer 15 minutes. Add cream and reduce to sauce-like consistency, cooking over medium heat. If desired, adjust consistency by gradually adding enough of the cornstarch slurry to taste. Season with salt and pepper to taste.

Cook linguine al dente in a large amount of boiling, salted water. Drain. Heat sauce, add reserved clams—either in or out of the shell—and toss with linguine, adding remaining parsley. Serve in warm bowls.

ORECCHIETTE PASTA WITH PANCETTA, CABBAGE, AND ITALIAN CHEESE

Yield: 8 generous servings

---

3 ounces pancetta, cut in small strips or diced (about 1 cup)
Olive oil as needed
3–4 cups cabbage, cut in julienne and diced
2 cloves garlic, minced
Salt and freshly ground pepper
½ cup dry white wine
½ cup chicken stock, plus more if needed
½ pound orecchiette pasta
¼ pound Fontina cheese
½ cup Parmigiano-Reggiano cheese
¼ cup heavy cream (optional), or more if desired

In a large skillet, sauté pancetta until fat has rendered. If the pancetta is very lean, add 1 to 2 tablespoons olive oil. Toss in cabbage and garlic and cook until soft. During some of the cooking time, you might wish to cover the pan. Add salt and freshly ground pepper to taste, being careful not to overseason since pancetta is salty.

Add white wine and deglaze pan. When wine has reduced, add chicken broth. Cook an additional few minutes to blend. Set aside.

Cook orecchiette al dente in salted boiling water for about 10 minutes. Drain. Toss the pasta with the sauce and add Fontina and Parmesan cheeses. Toss well and add cream, if desired. Mix again and serve at once in warm bowls or on heated plates.

Pasta Mafalda

*L*ong before I started cooking seriously, I always enjoyed going to the Park Schenley for Pasta Mafalda, a specialty of the restaurant. The pasta is a simple dish relying on the quality and flavor of the cheeses and tomato sauce, with an elegant touch of cream. With proper ingredients on hand, in 30 minutes you will have created a memorable pasta dish.

Yield: 4–6 servings

¾ pound pappardelle pasta
2 tablespoons extra-virgin olive oil
Salt and freshly ground pepper
1½ cups grated Romano cheese
2 cups homemade tomato sauce (warm or at room temperature)
½ cup heavy cream, or to taste
Freshly grated Parmigiano-Reggiano cheese

Cook pasta al dente (tender to the bite) in a large pot of boiling, salted water. Drain in a colander but do not rinse. Return pasta to pot and over low heat add olive oil, salt, freshly ground pepper, and Romano cheese, tossing to coat pasta evenly. Add tomato sauce and then cream, mixing well. Serve as soon as pasta and sauce are hot and cream has slightly reduced. Finish each serving with a sprinkling of freshly grated Parmigiano-Reggiano cheese.

Spaghetti all'Ortolana

Yield: 4–6 servings

1 medium eggplant
Salt
Olive oil as needed
1 tablespoon finely chopped garlic
½ cup chopped flat-leaf parsley
2 cups peeled and chopped tomatoes
Hot red pepper flakes to taste
¾ pound spaghetti

Cut off the ends of the eggplant and discard. Cut eggplant into ¼-inch rounds, generously salt, and place in a colander to drain about 30 minutes. Squeeze eggplant slices with a towel to remove most of the moisture.

Add about ¼ inch of olive oil to a nonstick skillet and, when hot, cook the slices of eggplant, being sure not to crowd the pan, until golden brown, adding more oil if necessary. Drain cooked slices on paper towels.

Heat about 4 tablespoons olive oil in a second skillet and add the garlic, cooking briefly. Add chopped parsley, tomatoes, and hot pepper flakes and simmer, uncovered, about 20 minutes.

Using a large pot, bring salted water to a boil and cook spaghetti al dente, approximately 5 minutes.

Meanwhile, cut the eggplant slices into thin strips. Add the strips to the sauce and cook about 3 minutes. Serve tossed with spaghetti in warm bowls or on plates and pass freshly grated Parmesan cheese and additional hot pepper flakes.

FISH AND SEAFOOD

BROILED BLACK SEA BASS ANGLAISE
76

ASIAN GRILLED SALMON
77

BAKED SALMON WITH
SHIITAKE MUSHROOM CRUST
78

BOURRIDE
80

CHA CA
83

ESCABECHE
85

CIOPPINO
87

SEARED TUNA WITH WASABI MAYONNAISE
AND ASIAN COUSCOUS SALAD
88

STEAMED HALIBUT WITH CRISPY SHALLOTS
AND WARM LEEK VINAIGRETTE
90

BROILED BLACK SEA BASS ANGLAISE

*M*y very favorite fish recipe uses black sea bass, a mild white fish with a firm but delicate texture. The fish may be broiled, sautéed, or panfried; I prefer broiling. I first dredge the fish with flour, then brush with melted butter seasoned with Tabasco and paprika. The flour works as a sealer and the butter mixture accentuates the flavor. "Anglaise" is an English term implying the use of moistened, seasoned breadcrumbs as an attractive topping to provide another textural dimension.

Yield: 8 servings

8 fish fillets (black sea bass preferred), approximately 5 ounces each
½ cup flour
3 tablespoons butter
Liberal dash Tabasco sauce
Paprika
Salt to taste

Dredge fish fillets with flour. Melt butter and oil in a small pan. Off heat, season with Tabasco sauce and add paprika. Mix well. Brush flour-coated fish with mixture on both sides, season with salt, and place on broiling pan. Do not use rack. Refrigerate until ready to use.

TOPPING:

1 cup fresh breadcrumbs
2 cloves garlic, minced or crushed
¼ cup finely chopped flat-leaf parsley
2–3 tablespoons olive oil (enough to moisten but not saturate crumbs)

Combine breadcrumbs, minced or crushed garlic, and parsley in a small bowl. Add enough olive oil to moisten crumbs. Reserve.

Preheat broiler.

Broil according to size of fish, usually not more than 4 to 5 minutes. It is not necessary to turn fish. About 1 minute before fish is done, sprinkle with topping and broil until nicely and lightly browned.

Between the lines: I use good-quality packaged white bread, such as Pepperidge Farm. Use a blender or food processor to make breadcrumbs. Surplus fresh breadcrumbs should be stored in the freezer.

ASIAN GRILLED SALMON

Asian flavors, especially soy sauce, partner well with salmon. Salmon may be grilled or broiled, but whichever way you choose, to retain moisture and a delicious velvety texture, do not overcook.

Yield: 8 servings

1 side of salmon, skin removed (about 1½–2 pounds)
¼ cup dry sherry
¼ cup reduced-sodium soy sauce
2 tablespoons oyster sauce
2 tablespoons lemon juice
2 tablespoons Asian sesame oil
Freshly ground pepper
2 tablespoons minced shallot
¼ cup minced fresh ginger
1 tablespoon olive or vegetable oil

Remove any bones from salmon fillet with tweezers and cut into 8 pieces.

Combine all remaining ingredients except cooking oil and marinate salmon pieces 30 minutes at room temperature. Reserve marinade.

continued

Preheat a stovetop grill until hot. Brush grill with a paper towel and small amount of cooking oil and grill salmon, turning once, 2 to 3 minutes per side, depending on thickness of salmon and personal taste. While salmon is cooking, heat reserved marinade in a small pot, reduce until slightly thickened, and brush over salmon when done.

Between the lines: If you choose to broil the salmon, do not turn it. It is not necessary to turn fish when using an oven broiler or stovetop grill. I am very partial to a stovetop grill and use it for grilling fish, vegetables, and sometimes boneless chicken breasts.

BAKED SALMON
WITH SHIITAKE MUSHROOM CRUST

I learned this recipe from a chef at ZD Wines in Napa Valley in the early 1980s. Shirley was talented and creative, and when she left to open her own bed-and-breakfast, I lost a valuable cooking resource. Baked Salmon with Shiitake Mushroom Crust is a perfect choice for entertaining, since the salmon may be prepared ahead and baked when needed. Actually, the dish is equally delicious when baked ahead and served at room temperature.

Yield: 8–10 servings

---

3 tablespoons extra-virgin olive oil
2 shallots, minced
½ pound shiitake mushrooms, stems removed, coarsely chopped
Salt and freshly ground pepper
2 tablespoons finely chopped fresh thyme
2 cups fresh breadcrumbs*
Additional splash of olive oil
1 whole salmon fillet, skin and bones removed (2½–3 pounds)
2–3 tablespoons Dijon mustard (enough to coat the top of the salmon)

---

*To make breadcrumbs, use Pepperidge Farm or other quality white bread. Process bread into crumbs in a food processor.

Heat olive oil in a medium frying pan. Add shallots and sauté 2 minutes. Add mushrooms and continue cooking until mushrooms are soft. Season with salt, freshly ground pepper, and thyme. Mixture should be dry.

Turn mushrooms into a bowl, combine with breadcrumbs, and add enough olive oil to lightly bind mixture.

Preheat oven to 400 degrees.

Place salmon on a baking sheet. Brush top with Dijon mustard and season with salt and freshly ground pepper. Spread mushroom-crumb mixture evenly over top of salmon and bake at 400 degrees about 15 minutes. To brown crust, place under hot broiler for 10 to 15 seconds.

Between the lines: Whenever possible, try to buy salmon in season. Look for wild salmon that has not been frozen. Farm-raised salmon can be used, but it lacks the flavor and texture of a seasonal fish.

BOURRIDE

*M*y husband and I first tasted Bourride in Golfe Juan, a small village on the French Riviera. Bourride incorporates the marvelous flavors of the South of France and is somewhere between a fish stew and a soup. Adding croutons and a dollop of zesty aioli gives the perfect finish.

Yield: 6–8 servings

---

3 tablespoons good-quality olive oil
1 cup chopped onions
¾ cup chopped leeks
¾ cup sliced fennel
1–2 tablespoons toasted ground fennel seed
½ cup chopped celery
1 tablespoon minced garlic
Saffron to taste (about ¼ teaspoon powdered; 1 teaspoon threads)
1 bay leaf
1 tablespoon fresh thyme, or 1 teaspoon dried
1 cup dry white wine
6 cups Fish Stock (p. 82)
1 pound small new potatoes, sliced into thin rounds
Salt and freshly ground pepper to taste
¼ teaspoon dried red pepper flakes
1 pound fish fillets, such as halibut, red snapper, grouper, or monkfish, cut into cubes
    or thick slices
Garlic Croutons
Aioli
Cornstarch slurry (1 tablespoon cornstarch dissolved in 2 tablespoons cold water), optional

---

Heat the olive oil in a large saucepan over medium-high heat and add the onions, leeks, fennel, fennel seed, celery, and garlic. Cook over medium heat until soft, about 5 minutes. Add dissolved saffron, bay leaf, and thyme, blend, and cook 2 minutes. Add wine, fish broth, potatoes, salt, pepper, and hot pepper flakes. Bring to a boil, lower heat, and simmer, covered, 30 minutes.

Pass ingredients through a food mill into a clean saucepan large enough to hold soup and fish. If sauce is too thick, thin with stock or a little wine. Add fish, being sure not to crowd pan, and bring to a boil, lower heat, and cook 3 minutes at a simmer. Using a slotted spoon, transfer fish to warm serving bowls. Add 2 or 3 croutons to each bowl and spoon Aioli over each crouton. Pour hot broth over all and serve.

If sauce seems too thin, thicken with cornstarch slurry added gradually to simmering sauce until desired consistency is reached.

GARLIC CROUTONS

1 baguette or small loaf French or Italian bread
4–5 cloves garlic
½ cup olive oil
Freshly ground pepper

Preheat oven to 325 degrees.

Combine garlic and olive oil. Cut bread into ½-inch slices and brush one side lightly with oil. Grind black pepper lightly over top. Place bread slices on baking sheet and toast in oven 20 minutes, until lightly browned.

AIOLI

1 tablespoon minced garlic
1 tablespoon Dijon mustard
1 large egg yolk, at room temperature
Salt and freshly ground pepper
Cayenne to taste
1 cup extra-virgin or good-quality olive oil

Place minced garlic in a small mixing bowl, add mustard, and blend. Add egg yolk and seasonings and whisk together. Continue whisking and slowly add olive oil in a steady stream, beating until all oil is incorporated and the aioli is smooth and thick.

continued

Between the lines: Bourride works well for dinner parties, since the base, croutons, and aioli may be prepared ahead. When ready to serve, reheat base and add the fish; the final cooking will be done in a matter of minutes. Serve in a large shallow bowl and pass croutons and aioli.

When using saffron, buy the best quality available, preferably from Spain. Saffron is expensive. I prefer the powder to the threads, but powdered saffron is not easy to come by. I brought my "stash" home from the market in Cannes. Avoid less-expensive saffron from India or the Middle East. In the case of saffron, you get what you pay for.

FISH STOCK

3–4 fish frames, with trimmings and heads (frames cut, heads cleaned)
2 onions, coarsely chopped
2 stalks celery, coarsely chopped
1 leek, coarsely chopped
6 peppercorns
3 cloves garlic, smashed
1 bouquet garni (bay leaf, sprigs of parsley, and thyme)
1 cup dry white wine
Water to cover (about 3 quarts)

Place frames, fish trimmings, and heads in a large pot with onions, celery, leek, peppercorns, garlic, bouquet garni, wine, and water. Slowly bring to a boil, then boil 1-minute, skimming scum and foam from surface. Lower heat to a simmer, and cook, partially covered, for 30 minutes. (It is important not to cook fish stock longer than 30 minutes, or it will become bitter.) Cool. Strain mixture through cheesecloth.

Fish stock may be frozen.

CHA CA

In 1994, my sister, my husband, and I went to Vietnam. Our first Vietnamese meal was at Cha Ca, the famous fish restaurant in Hanoi. A charcoal brazier was placed in the center of the table, followed by a rapid succession of bowls containing rice noodles, a local green resembling watercress, sliced onions, cilantro, warm peanuts, and *nuoc cham*, the seasoning sauce served with every Vietnamese meal. A young waitress placed a large frying pan of sizzling golden brown fish on the brazier and left. We puzzled over how to eat the fish. At the next table, an elderly man sensed our predicament and came to our aid. He filled our bowls with noodles, stirred greens into the pan with the fish, heating only long enough to soften the greens, then served the fish over the noodles, garnishing with onions, cilantro, peanuts, and sauce. Our first meal in Vietnam was undoubtedly our best, and it characterized the cooking and flavors of exotic Vietnam.

Yield: 4 servings

---

1 pound mild white fish (gray sole, snapper, sea bass, or other fish that can be fried)
Rice flour to coat fish
Vegetable oil (to the depth of ¼ inch in a large frying pan)
Greens (Swiss chard)
1 large mild white onion, sliced
1 bunch fresh cilantro, leaves and small stems chopped
1 bunch scallions, thinly sliced
Warm peanuts
Rice vermicelli

Dredge fish with rice flour and fry on both sides in hot oil. Push fish to the side of pan or place on a plate. Add coarsely cut Swiss chard greens and sauté a few minutes to soften.

Arrange sliced onions, cilantro, scallions, and peanuts in separate dishes. Cook rice vermicelli according to directions, then toss with onions. Place mixture in a bowl, top with fish and greens, then sprinkle with cilantro, scallions, and warm peanuts. Serve with the following sauce, a version of the Vietnamese *nuoc cham*.

continued

Spicy Fish Sauce

2 small cloves garlic, crushed
1 small fresh red chile pepper, seeded and minced
2 tablespoons sugar
2 tablespoons fresh lime juice
¼ cup rice vinegar
¼ cup Vietnamese fish sauce (*nuoc mam*) or Thai fish sauce (*nam pla*)

Combine all ingredients, blend well, and serve with fish.

ESCABECHE

I first saw Escabeche made with mackerel in one of Michael Field's cookbooks. Escabeche is Spanish, and is a method for pickling fish. Field was a master cook, way ahead of his time, and unfortunately died all too young. His recipes are classic. Escabeche is an excellent example and a good choice for warm weather dining. The finished dish is colorful and a beauty to behold. Serve at room temperature.

Yield: 8–10 servings

---

2 eggs
2 tablespoons milk
1¼ pounds sole or flounder, seasoned with salt and pepper and cut into 2x4-inch pieces
½ cup good-quality olive oil (non-boutique extra-virgin)
1 cup sliced onions (preferably white)
1 cup peeled and sliced carrots
1 cup peeled, seeded, and sliced red and yellow peppers
5 cloves garlic, thinly sliced
2–3 teaspoons salt
2 bay leaves
Few sprigs of fresh thyme, or ½ teaspoon dried
10 whole peppercorns
1 cup cold water
½ cup white wine vinegar
1 cup dried breadcrumbs
Vegetable or peanut oil

GARNISH

¼ cup Niçoise or other black olives
¼ cup finely chopped parsley
Thin lemon slices

---

continued

Combine eggs and milk in a bowl or pie plate and blend well. Add seasoned fish strips and refrigerate 1 to 2 hours.

Heat olive oil in a deep saucepan. Add onions, carrots, peppers, and garlic and sauté over low heat 3 to 5 minutes. Add salt, bay leaves, thyme, and peppercorns, then cold water and wine vinegar. Bring to a boil, lower heat, and simmer, covered, 12 minutes. (This can be done ahead.)

Spread breadcrumbs on a plate and coat each piece of fish. (This may also be done in a paper bag.) In a large frying pan, heat approximately ½ inch vegetable or peanut oil. When hot, brown fish pieces, turning once. Browning takes 1 to 2 minutes if oil is hot enough. Drain fish on paper towels, salt lightly, and arrange in shallow dish. Ladle warm marinade and vegetables artfully over fish. When cool, chill in the refrigerator until cold.

To serve: Garnish with black olives and sprinkle with parsley. Add lemon garnish just before serving. Fish may be served cold or at room temperature and may successfully be prepared a day ahead.

CIOPPINO

Cioppino, a hearty fisherman's stew using a tomato base, originated in San Francisco. It was probably first served at some local Italian restaurant on Fisherman's Wharf. The base should be made ahead, and the fish and seafood added for the last few minutes of cooking. Flavorful and enhanced with fresh fish and seafood, Cioppino offers a satisfying one-dish meal. The only accompaniment necessary is a loaf of fresh sourdough bread.

Yield: 10 servings

---

1 cup chopped green bell pepper
1½ cups finely chopped onion
1–2 jalapeño peppers, seeded and finely chopped
⅓ cup olive oil
6 cups chopped Italian-style tomatoes, including juices
2 tablespoons tomato paste
2 cups dry red wine
2 teaspoons dried oregano
2 teaspoons dried thyme, or 1 tablespoon fresh
¼ cup chopped fresh basil
1 bay leaf
¾ pound shrimp (about 18)
2 dozen clams in the shell
1½ pounds halibut or scrod, cut into 1½-inch pieces
¾ pound sea scallops
½ cup finely chopped parsley

In a kettle or deep pot, cook the green pepper, onion, and jalapeño pepper in the olive oil over low heat, stirring occasionally, until vegetables are softened. Add the tomatoes, tomato paste, wine, and herbs. Bring liquid to a boil and cook at a simmer, covered, for 1 hour.

continued

While the mixture is cooking, shell shrimp, leaving tails on, and cut down the back to butterfly and devein.

Remove the lid from the sauce, bring mixture to a boil, and stir in the clams. Boil uncovered, transferring clams to a bowl as they open. Taste the sauce for seasoning; add the shrimp, halibut or scrod, and sea scallops, cooking the seafood 4 to 5 minutes. Place clams in the shell in shallow soup bowls and add sauce, giving each serving a sampling of the fish and shellfish. Garnish with chopped parsley.

Seared Tuna with Wasabi Mayonnaise and Asian Couscous Salad

No set of fish recipes would be complete without a version of seared tuna. I am partial to this recipe because the Wasabi Mayonnaise highlights the tuna, and the Asian Couscous Salad is a perfect and satisfying accompaniment.

Yield: 8 appetizer servings

1-pound piece loin of tuna
2–3 tablespoons extra-virgin olive oil
1 teaspoon salt
2 teaspoons coarsely cracked black and/or white peppercorns

Heat a 10-inch cast-iron skillet until very hot, about 15 minutes.

Cut tuna loin into 4x1½-inch blocks. Brush the blocks on all sides with olive oil. Season with salt and dredge with cracked peppercorns. When pan is ready, sear tuna blocks 30 to 45 seconds per side. You can watch the progress of the searing by the dark border that forms on the four sides around the edge. You want a very narrow border. Transfer to plate, cover loosely with foil, and refrigerate until ready to serve.

Wasabi Mayonnaise

1 egg yolk
1 tablespoon rice vinegar or 1 teaspoon lemon juice
2 teaspoons wasabi paste or to taste
½ cup grapeseed or vegetable oil
A few drops lemon oil or finely grated lemon rind to taste

Combine egg yolk, rice vinegar or lemon juice, and wasabi paste in a bowl and whisk to combine. Add grapeseed or vegetable oil a few drops at a time to form an emulsion, then add oil in a thin stream, whisking continually, to make a thick mayonnaise. Adjust seasonings.

Asian Couscous Salad

1 cup couscous
1½ cups boiling water

Measure couscous into a bowl. Pour boiling water over couscous and cover. Couscous will absorb water in about 5 minutes and be ready to use.

2–3 medium-sized plum tomatoes, peeled, seeded, and cut into small dice
1 bunch scallions, sliced into very thin rings (white bulbs and tender green tops)
1 cup peeled, seeded, and finely diced cucumber
½ cup peeled, seeded, and finely diced red, orange, or green bell pepper
1 avocado, peeled and cut into small dice

Combine couscous with tomatoes, scallions, cucumber, pepper, and avocado.

Asian Dressing

3 tablespoons rice vinegar
Salt and freshly ground pepper
4 tablespoons extra-virgin olive oil
Sesame oil to taste
½ cup chopped fresh mint

continued

Whisk ingredients together for Asian Dressing, except mint, and combine with couscous. Taste for seasoning and finish by adding chopped mint.

Mold a serving of couscous in a small (3-ounce) ramekin. Turn out onto an individual plate. Slice tuna, arrange on plate, and drizzle mayonnaise over tuna. Repeat for each appetizer plate using the same ramekin for molding.

STEAMED HALIBUT WITH CRISPY SHALLOTS AND WARM LEEK VINAIGRETTE

genuine "twofer," this recipe is delicious served "à la minute" and wonderful the next day redesigned as a chilled seafood salad. The simplicity of this dish calls for quality fresh fish and the best extra-virgin olive oil.

Yield: 6 servings

Corn (or other vegetable) oil poured ¾ inch up the sides of a small skillet
1½ cups shallots, sliced into thin rings
1 bunch leeks (white part) cut lengthwise, rinsed, and cut into ¾-inch dice (2½–3 cups)
Salt and freshly ground pepper to taste

Heat oil in a small skillet and, when hot (but not smoking), brown shallot rings in small batches, until golden. To finish browning, it may be necessary to add more oil. Remove with a slotted spoon and drain on paper towels. Salt lightly. Set aside.

Fill a medium-sized bowl with a handful of ice cubes and water. Bring a medium-sized pot of salted water to the boil and blanch leeks 3 to 4 minutes. Drain and immediately immerse leeks in ice water. After 5 minutes, drain again and dry in paper towels.

Vinaigrette

1 tablespoon sherry wine vinegar
1 tablespoon red wine vinegar
1–2 teaspoons balsamic vinegar
½ cup extra-virgin olive oil
Salt and freshly ground pepper
3 tablespoons minced flat-leaf parsley

Prepare vinaigrette by combining sherry, red wine, and balsamic vinegars and olive oil in a small bowl. Add salt and pepper to taste. In a sauté pan, over medium-high heat, combine leeks and vinaigrette and heat 2 minutes. Add parsley and reserve.

To prepare halibut:

1½ pounds halibut cut into 6 portions (approximately 4 ounces each)
1 cup stringed snow peas

Season both sides of halibut with salt and freshly ground pepper to taste. Place on a steamer rack with snow peas arranged around the fish. Cover and steam over gently boiling water until fish is opaque, about 4 to 5 minutes. Do not allow water to touch fish.

To serve warm: Reheat leek vinaigrette. Place a spoonful on each plate, and then arrange a piece of halibut and some snow peas on top of leeks. Scatter fried shallots over top and serve.

To serve cold: Flake cooked halibut. Combine with snow peas (cut in diagonals). Mix well with vinaigrette. Chill. When ready to serve, top with crispy fried shallots.

POULTRY

BREAST OF CHICKEN AU POIVRE
94

BREAST OF CHICKEN PROVENÇALE
95

BREAST OF CHICKEN WITH MARSALA WINE
AND EXOTIC MUSHROOMS
96

CHICKEN MILANESE
98

MAGRET DE CANARD
WITH CRANBERRY CASSIS SAUCE
99

FRICASSEE OF CHICKEN PROVENÇALE
101

ROSEMARY ROAST CHICKEN
102

BREAST OF CHICKEN AU POIVRE

I like to serve this dish to company, because it is easy to prepare and may be made ahead and reheated on top of the stove. In preparing the chicken breasts, remove the small fillet and cut out the tough white tendon from each fillet. Fillets may be wrapped and frozen and may be used in stir-fries or other recipes requiring small pieces of chicken.

Yield: 8 servings

4 large chicken breasts, boned, skinned, and split
Salt and freshly ground pepper
4 tablespoons butter
1 cup thinly sliced onions
1 cup diced carrots
½ cup diced celery
½ cup sliced leeks (white part)
1 tablespoon minced garlic
Bouquet garni (parsley, bay leaf, and thyme)
2 tablespoons flour
¾ cup dry vermouth or dry white wine
2 cups chicken stock
1 tablespoon Dijon mustard
Heavy cream (use ¼–½ cup to taste)
2 tablespoons green peppercorns, smashed

Season chicken breasts with salt and pepper.

Melt butter in a large frying pan and add onions, carrots, celery, leeks, and garlic. Cook, covered, 10 minutes without browning.

Arrange chicken breasts on top of vegetables and add bouquet garni. Cover and cook, turning once, until chicken is no longer translucent, about 5 to 8 minutes.

Remove chicken to side plate, blend in 2 tablespoons flour, and add vermouth and chicken stock. Blend. Cover and cook at a simmer 25 minutes. Strain, return sauce to clean pan, and add mustard, blending well. Add cream and heat sauce, reducing to sauce-like consistency over medium heat. Add peppercorns.

Reheat chicken breasts in sauce and serve.

Breast of Chicken Provençale

Breast of Chicken Provençale is another dish that works well for company dinners. Almost everybody enjoys chicken, and when combined with the flavors of Provence, this recipe is a sure winner.

Yield: 8 servings

---

4 large chicken breasts (about 1 pound each), boned, skinned, and cut in half
Salt and freshly ground pepper
½ cup flour
1 tablespoon olive oil
1 tablespoon butter
¼ cup chopped shallots
1 tablespoon minced garlic
1 cup chopped tomatoes
1 tablespoon finely chopped fresh thyme, or 1 teaspoon dried
½ cup dry white wine
¼ cup Madeira wine
3 cups chicken stock, divided
Butter as needed, begin with 4 tablespoons
¾ pound sliced fresh mushrooms of your choice
1 tablespoon tomato paste
Cornstarch slurry (1 tablespoon cornstarch dissolved in 2 tablespoons cold stock or water), if needed

---

continued

Season chicken pieces with salt and pepper. Dredge with flour. Heat olive oil and butter in a large skillet and when hot, add chicken pieces, being sure not to crowd pan. Sauté until nicely browned, turning once. Reserve on side plate.

Add shallots, garlic, and more oil if necessary and sauté a few minutes, until soft but not brown. Add tomatoes and thyme, stir to combine, and cook a few minutes. Add white wine and Madeira and reduce by half over moderately high heat. Add 2 cups of the chicken stock and simmer, covered, 15 minutes. Pass sauce through strainer and reserve.

In a clean frying pan, heat 4 tablespoons butter. Sauté mushrooms, seasoning with salt and pepper, and cook 4 to 5 minutes, adding more butter if necessary. Add remaining cup of chicken stock, tomato paste, and reduce by half over moderately high heat. Combine mushrooms and prior sauce and, if too thin, thicken with cornstarch slurry, added gradually to simmering sauce until desired consistency is reached. Return chicken to pan, cover, and simmer 10 minutes, or until heated through.

Note: If there is too much acid in sauce, modify with a small amount of currant jelly or honey (1 to 2 teaspoons to taste).

Breast of Chicken with Marsala Wine and Exotic Mushrooms

Yield: 10 servings

1 ounce dried porcini mushrooms (about 1 cup loosely packed)
Salt and freshly ground pepper
5 chicken breasts, boned, skinned, and split (10 pieces, each about 6–8 ounces)
½ cup flour
4 tablespoons unsalted butter, or half butter and half olive oil
½ cup dry Marsala wine
½ cup dry white wine
3 cups chicken stock, divided
½ cup reserved porcini soaking liquid
Cornstarch slurry (2 teaspoons cornstarch dissolved in 2 tablespoons cold water or stock), if needed

Soak dried porcini mushrooms in 2 cups hot water for 20 minutes. Lift out mushrooms, rinse, and drain. Pass soaking liquid through a strainer lined with a wet paper towel. Reserve strained liquid. You will use ½ cup in cooking the chicken and maybe more later.

Salt and pepper split chicken breasts and dredge with flour. Melt butter in a large sauté pan and, when hot, add only enough chicken pieces to comfortably fit in the pan. Do not crowd. Cook chicken in two batches. Sauté over moderately high heat until brown on one side, turn, and brown second side. Remove to side plate and season lightly with salt.

Add the Marsala wine to pan, scraping bottom to loosen brown bits. Add the white wine and 2 cups of the chicken stock. Reduce by one-third over high heat. Add the remaining cup of chicken stock and ½ cup reserved mushroom soaking liquid and cook an additional few minutes. Return chicken breasts to pan (this time you may place them close together), bring sauce to a boil, lower heat, cover, and cook 15 minutes at a simmer.

Remove chicken breasts to a plate. Cook sauce over moderately high heat to reduce slightly and, if desired, thicken with a cornstarch slurry added gradually to the simmering sauce.

TO FINISH DISH:

---

4 tablespoons butter
¾–1 pound "exotic" fresh mushrooms (shiitake, oyster, cremini), wiped with a damp
   paper towel, sliced or quartered
Reserved porcini mushrooms
Splash olive oil
Salt and freshly ground pepper
1 tablespoon chopped fresh thyme
⅓ cup dry Marsala wine
1 cup chicken stock

Melt butter in a large frying pan and, when hot, add the fresh and porcini mushrooms in batches and sauté over moderately high heat 4 to 5 minutes. Add a splash of olive oil, season with salt and freshly ground pepper, add thyme, and mix well. Add Marsala wine and cook 2 to 3 minutes. Place chicken breasts in the pan sauce is in and arrange mushrooms over top.

Deglaze frying pan in which mushrooms were cooked with the chicken stock, reducing by half, and drizzle over mushrooms. Reheat, covered, on top of the stove.

Chicken Milanese

Yield: 8 servings

---

4 split chicken breasts, skinned, boned, and cut in half
Salt and freshly ground pepper
½ cup flour
2 eggs, beaten with 2 tablespoons water
2 cups fresh breadcrumbs combined with 1 cup freshly grated Parmesan cheese
1 stick unsalted butter, clarified*
½ cup dry white wine
1 cup chicken stock
Additional butter to taste (optional)
½ pound fresh mushrooms, thinly sliced
1 red bell pepper, peeled and cut into julienne
Peel of 1 lemon, blanched and cut into julienne
Finely chopped parsley

Pound the pieces of chicken breast to flatten slightly. Season with salt and pepper and dust each piece with flour, then dip pieces into egg and water mixture. Roll pieces in combined breadcrumbs and cheese, place on cookie sheet, and lightly cover with waxed paper.

In a large frying pan, add enough butter to cover the bottom of the pan to a depth of between ¼ and ½ inch. When butter is hot, brown chicken pieces on each side. Place finished pieces in a serving dish and keep warm.

Pour off excess butter. Deglaze pan with the wine. Add chicken stock and cook over moderately high heat, reducing contents to about 1 cup. If desired, add 1 to 2 tablespoons chilled butter to enrich and lightly thicken sauce.

Add mushrooms, lower heat, and incorporate in sauce. Add red pepper and lemon julienne and cook another 2 minutes. With a spatula, spread mixture evenly over chicken and top with finely chopped parsley.

*To clarify butter: Melt butter over very low heat. Remove foam from top and pour off clear liquid, discarding milk solids on the bottom. Though it is not mandatory to refrigerate clarified butter, I prefer keeping it in the refrigerator.

Magret de Canard
with Cranberry Cassis Sauce

*C*ranberries, so traditional around the holidays, complement duck quite well and make for an interesting variation on classic Magret of Duck. I would think rhubarb, too, would partner well with duck when cranberries are out of season. Crème de Cassis, made from black currants, is available here too and often used to add a touch of fruit to a glass of champagne in the aperitif Kir Royale. A raspberry-flavored liqueur, such as Framboise, will work quite well in place of the Cassis.

Yield: 8 servings

Magret

2 duck breasts (4 halves)
Quatre épices (cinnamon, ginger, clove, and nutmeg, finely ground)
Salt and freshly ground pepper
¼ cup Armagnac

Remove fat from duck breasts and cut each breast in half. Remove as much silver skin as possible. Season with quatre épices, salt, and freshly ground pepper. Place in shallow dish and cover with Armagnac. Marinate in the refrigerator or at room temperature, depending on how much time elapses between marinating and cooking. Breasts should marinate at room temperature up to 2 hours, and in the refrigerator up to 4 hours.

continued

CRANBERRY CASSIS SAUCE

1 package (12 ounces) fresh cranberries
1 cup cold water
¼ cup sugar
¼ cup Crème de Cassis
¼ cup finely chopped shallots
1½ cups dry red wine
Veal or excellent-quality chicken stock as needed (about 3 cups)
Few drops of honey

Cook cranberries in water until they pop open. Add sugar, stir to dissolve, then add Cassis and cook over low heat about 20 minutes.

Combine shallots and red wine in a saucepot and reduce by three-fourths. Add 1 cup veal or chicken stock and reduce by half over moderate heat. Add second cup of veal or chicken stock and about ½ cup Cranberry Cassis Sauce and cook until slightly thickened. Taste, and if too tart, soften flavor with a few drops of honey. Strain and put aside.

To cook magret:

4 tablespoons butter
¼ cup Armagnac
Veal stock or chicken stock
Base sauce
1–2 tablespoons butter

Melt butter in a large frying pan, add duck breasts, and sauté, turning once. Cook about 7 to 8 minutes total. Heat Armagnac in a small pot, ignite, and slowly add to pan, being sure to do this in an open area and away from your face. Remove breasts to a board, cover with a lid to finish cooking, and let rest for 10 minutes.

Add 1 cup veal or chicken stock to pan and deglaze. Add sauce and reduce over moderate heat until sauce-like consistency. Pour juices that have accumulated from duck into sauce. Adjust seasoning and, if desired, add 1 to 2 tablespoons chilled butter for added richness. Slice duck thin and serve with sauce.

Fricassee of Chicken Provençale

Yield: 8 servings

¾ pound hot or sweet sausage, or a combination
4 large chicken breasts, boned, split, and skin removed
Salt and freshly ground pepper
½ cup flour
Olive oil (6–8 tablespoons)
2 medium onions, cut into large dice
4 cloves garlic, thinly sliced
2 red and/or yellow bell peppers, peeled and cut into large dice (2–3 cups)
1 small eggplant, cut into dice
1 cup red or white wine
3 cups chicken stock
½–1 cup tomato sauce
Cornstarch slurry (1 tablespoon cornstarch dissolved in 2 tablespoons water), optional

---

Bring a pot of water large enough to hold sausage to a boil. Blanch sausages at a simmer for 5 minutes. Cool, remove casing, and cut into small pieces.

Season chicken breasts with salt and pepper. Dredge with flour. Heat 3 to 4 tablespoons olive oil in a large skillet and brown chicken pieces on both sides. Remove to plate. In same pan, brown sausages. Do not rinse skillet; reserve until needed.

In second large skillet, heat 4 tablespoons olive oil and sauté onions and garlic 3 to 4 minutes. Add peppers, cook an additional few minutes, and then add eggplant. Cook vegetables until soft. Set aside.

Discard fat from first skillet and deglaze with 1 cup wine. Reduce by half. Add 3 cups chicken stock and tomato sauce and reduce by one-third. Taste for flavor. At this point, sauce may be further reduced or thickened by gradually adding cornstarch slurry to simmering sauce.

In a large pan or ovenproof dish, arrange chicken pieces; add vegetables, sausages, and sauce. Bring contents of pan to a simmer, cover, and cook an additional 20 minutes on top of the stove or in a preheated 350-degree oven.

Dish may be made ahead and reheated at serving time.

ROSEMARY ROAST CHICKEN

*M*any chefs believe that to test a chef's mettle, you should ask him or her to roast a chicken. Properly roasted chicken is golden brown, with crispy skin and meat that is flavorful and succulent. Rosemary Roast Chicken is enhanced with the addition of fresh rosemary and a mix of mushrooms, fresh and dried. When I was growing up, "chicken every Sunday" was a popular choice in the United States. Carl and our three sons liked nothing better, and to satisfy everyone (as to who got dark or white meat) I often roasted two chickens—choosing slightly smaller birds (3½ pounds)—to make everyone happy.

Yield: 6 servings

---

1 onion, quartered
5 cloves garlic (2 smashed, 3 minced)
2–3 sprigs of rosemary
1 large chicken (about 4 pounds)
Salt and freshly ground pepper
Butter as needed (about 6–9 tablespoons)
½ cup chopped fresh rosemary
2 cups sliced fresh wild mushrooms (cremini, shiitake, and chanterelle)
1 ounce dried porcini mushrooms, soaked in 1½ cups hot water
1 cup dry white wine
3 cups good-quality chicken stock
Reserved and strained porcini soaking liquid, optional
Cornstarch slurry (1 tablespoon cornstarch dissolved in 2 to 3 tablespoons cold stock,
    mushroom liquid, or water), optional

Preheat oven to 425 degrees (400 degrees in convection oven). Preheat roasting pan in oven while preparing chicken.

Place onion quarters, smashed garlic, and rosemary sprigs in cavity of chicken. Sprinkle cavity with salt and freshly ground pepper. Gently loosen skin of chicken with your fingers, using a small knife when necessary. Push your fingers gently under the skin, working to free the breast, thighs, and legs from the skin.

Combine 6 to 8 tablespoons softened butter, minced garlic, and chopped rosemary well and with your fingers, evenly insert seasoned butter under skin. Smooth by pressing with your fingers on the outside of the skin. Tie the chicken with string and season exterior of the bird with salt and pepper.

When using a convection oven, simply place chicken in pan breast side up. Roast for 55 to 60 minutes without turning, basting a few times with fat and juices accumulated in the pan.

If using a standard oven, place preheated roasting pan in a 425-degree oven 20 minutes. Place chicken on one side and roast for 20 minutes, then turn chicken on other side and roast an additional 20 minutes. Finish by placing chicken breast side up and roast 15 to 20 minutes, basting every 5 minutes with juices accumulated in pan. Bird should be golden brown. Remove chicken from oven and place on cutting board. Do not wash roasting pan. Cover loosely with foil and allow chicken to rest up to a half hour before carving.

While chicken is roasting, prepare mushrooms. Rinse porcini mushrooms; pass soaking liquid through a strainer lined with cheesecloth or wet paper towel and reserve. Cut porcini in smaller pieces, if necessary.

Drain all but 2 to 3 tablespoons of fat from roasting pan. Place pan on burner over medium heat and add 1 tablespoon of butter. When butter and fat are hot, add fresh mushrooms and porcini and sauté for 3 minutes. Add 1 cup of wine and deglaze pan, scraping brown bits loose with a spatula. Reduce to about one-third. Add 2 cups of chicken stock and reduce by half. Add final cup of stock, and some mushroom soaking liquid, if desired, and cook a few more minutes, until desired consistency is reached.

At this point, sauce may be thickened with a cornstarch slurry added gradually to simmering stock until desired consistency is reached.

Carve chicken into serving pieces. Arrange on individual plates or platter and nap with sauce and mushrooms.

Meat

ELYSIAN FIELDS PARMESAN-BREADED
BABY LAMB CHOPS
106

GLAZED VEAL SCALLOPS
ON A BED OF SPINACH
108

MICHAEL FIELD'S
GRILLED BUTTERFLIED LEG OF LAMB
109

OSSO BUCCO
112

RACK OF LAMB PERSILLADE
114

MOM'S MEAT LOAF
116

STEAK AU POIVRE
117

ROAST BEEF WITH YORKSHIRE PUDDING
AND HORSERADISH CREAM
118

VEAL SCALLOPS PARMESAN
120

Elysian Fields Parmesan-Breaded Baby Lamb Chops

*N*obody was happier than I was when we took the family to Cannes and rented an apartment on the Riviera for the month of July. Cooking in Cannes was cooking in paradise, what with the availability of fresh ingredients and regional products only a walk away. Inspiration from restaurants like Le Royal Gray and from young chefs like Jacques Chibois and Jacques Maximin found me spending as much time in my small kitchen as at the beach. I went as far as making my own veal stock! A family favorite was Parmesan-Breaded Baby Lamb Chops. The recipe is easy to do, and once again, you do not even need the sauce if you use delicious young lamb.

Yield: 8 servings (2 chops each)

---

16 single-rib lamb chops, bones frenched and trimmed of fat, cut ½-inch thick
Salt and freshly ground pepper
1 cup freshly grated Parmigiano-Reggiano cheese
2 cups fine fresh breadcrumbs
½ cup flour
2 eggs, beaten
Clarified butter*

For best results, buy a rack of lamb and have the butcher cut the rack into single chops and french the bones, reserving all trimmings if you plan to make a sauce.

Using meat pounder or extender with a flat bottom, gently flatten the meat. Season chops with salt and freshly ground pepper. Combine cheese and breadcrumbs. Dredge chops in flour, then in egg, and coat with crumb mixture, shaking off the excess. Transfer to a platter lined with wax paper. (Chops may be coated up to 1 hour in advance and held at room temperature or up to 4 hours in advance and refrigerated loosely covered with foil or paper. If refrigerated, bring to room temperature before cooking.)

Coat the bottom of a large frying pan with 3 to 4 tablespoons clarified butter and over moderately high heat, sauté lamb chops (do not crowd pan) until golden brown, turning once. This should take 3 to 4 minutes, or less than 2 minutes per side.

Transfer to a warm plate or platter and if desired, serve with a light pan sauce.

*To clarify butter: Place 1 stick of unsalted butter in a small saucepan. Heat until butter bubbles and foam rises to the top. Remove visible foam with a spoon, and then pour butter through cheesecloth, straining out milky sediment.

I recommend clarified butter for frying when you want to have a crust. It browns but does not burn. Clarified butter will keep at room temperature, but I prefer to store it in the refrigerator.

To make sauce:

Butter (2–3 tablespoons)
Reserved trimmings or additional lamb riblets, trimmed of fat and cut into small pieces
Port wine (about ½ cup)
Good-quality chicken stock (about 3–4 cups)
Cornstarch slurry

Heat 2 tablespoons butter in a frying pan. Add reserved trimmings, or some additional lamb riblets, and over moderate heat, brown trimmings well. Pour off excess fat and deglaze pan with ½ cup port wine. (This is best done without trimmings in pan.) Return trimmings to pan, add 2 cups stock, and cook, covered, over moderate heat about 30 minutes. Strain sauce, discard trimmings, and pour sauce into a clean frying pan, adding another cup of stock. Reduce over moderately high heat until sauce has thickened slightly (the consistency should be syrupy). A cornstarch slurry (1 tablespoon cornstarch dissolved in 3 tablespoons cold stock or water) may be gradually added to simmering sauce to reach desired consistency. Sauce may be made ahead, refrigerated, and reheated.

Glazed Veal Scallops on a Bed of Spinach

Here is a recipe from my early days of cooking, when veal was in fashion. This rendition is a variation on the many veal scaloppine dishes made and enjoyed at that time.

Yield: 8 servings

Butter as needed (at least 8 tablespoons)
2 packages (12 ounces each) fresh spinach, cleaned and dried
Salt and freshly ground pepper
1½ pounds veal scallops
¾ cup flour
⅓ cup Madeira wine
⅓ cup dry white wine
2 cups chicken stock
2 teaspoons tomato paste
½ pound Fontina cheese, sliced thin
¾ cup tomato sauce
½ cup Parmesan cheese (optional)

Heat 4 tablespoons butter in a large frying pan. Gradually add spinach and cook only until spinach wilts. Season with salt and freshly ground pepper, and place spinach in a single layer on the bottom of a gratin or shallow baking dish.

Season veal scallops with salt and pepper and dredge each one in flour, patting off excess.

Heat 4 tablespoons butter in the same frying pan, and when hot, sauté veal scallops on each side, until lightly browned. Place finished scallops on side plate.

Deglaze frying pan with ⅓ cup of each wine. Add chicken stock and tomato paste and cook over moderate heat, until sauce is somewhat reduced and lightly thickened.

Arrange veal scallops on spinach bed with a thin slice of cheese in between. Scallops should overlap. Pour sauce over scallops and spinach and dribble heated tomato sauce over top. If desired, finish with a liberal sprinkling of grated Parmesan cheese.

To serve: Bring to a simmer on top of the stove and heat through, then glaze under broiler until gratin is hot and bubbly.

Michael Field's
Grilled Butterflied Leg of Lamb

*M*ichael Field died at the age of fifty-eight, leaving only three or four cookbooks as his legacy. He was a gifted musician, as well as a maestro in the kitchen. His recipes are well written and, though sometimes lengthy, easy to follow. The results are superb. Grilled Butterflied Leg of Lamb has been made and enjoyed I don't know how many times in our home. For years, it was the centerpiece of our Passover Seder, and when I used it in my classes, it was a great favorite, especially with the men.

Yield: 10–12 servings

5–6 pound leg of lamb, boned

Ask the butcher to bone the leg of lamb. At home, place meat on a board, fat side down. The meat should lie flat. Cut through and separate any pockets of meat and remove any clumps of fat. You may wish to remove the small piece of attached meat that tends to be full of gristle.

Marinate the lamb for at least 12 hours, preferably 24, with the following marinade. Cover the meat with foil and refrigerate, removing to room temperature the last few hours.

continued

Marinade

⅔ cup good-quality olive oil
3 tablespoons lemon juice
1 teaspoon salt
½ teaspoon freshly ground black pepper
½ cup chopped flat-leaf parsley
1 tablespoon dried oregano
3 bay leaves, crumbled
1½ cups thinly sliced onions
4 cloves garlic, thinly sliced
Salt and coarsely ground pepper or Lawry's Seasoned Black, to season lamb

Combine olive oil, lemon juice, salt, pepper, parsley, oregano, and crumbled bay leaves in a large baking dish or pan. Mix in onions and garlic. Season both sides of meat with salt and pepper, place in pan with marinade, and turn meat to coat both sides. Turn meat every few hours or at least the last few hours at room temperature.

To grill meat: From start to finish, and using a preheated grill, the leg of lamb should take about 20 to 25 minutes to cook. Make sure grill has been preheated at least 15 minutes. Lift meat from marinade and lay it fat side down on hot grill, grids placed about 6 inches above heat. Cook meat 7 minutes, turn meat with a pair of tongs (not a fork), and moisten with a few tablespoons of marinade. Cook another 7 minutes and turn. Cook 4 minutes, turn, and finish with 2 more minutes of cooking. Ideally, the finished meat should be pale pink, rimmed with a dark brown crust, with a suggestion of red in the center. The thinner areas of the leg will be quite well done. In other words, there will be something for everybody—rare, pink, medium, and well done, depending on the section you are carving. You may want to press the thickest part of the lamb with your fingers. It should be firm to the touch. If the meat feels squishy, cook an additional 5 minutes.

Rest meat on a board for 20 minutes (you may cover lightly with foil) before carving. Carve the leg against the grain into thin slices. Moisten meat with any juices on board and serve on warmed plates. Pass the Avgolemono Sauce separately.

Avgolemono Sauce

3 egg yolks
1 tablespoon lemon juice
2 teaspoons cornstarch dissolved in 1 tablespoon cold stock or water
Salt and cayenne pepper to taste
1 cup chicken stock
2 tablespoons finely chopped parsley or fresh mint

In a sturdy, heavy-bottomed small pot, whisk the egg yolks, lemon juice, dissolved cornstarch, salt, and cayenne until well blended. Slowly stir in the chicken stock. Cook sauce over moderate heat, stirring continuously, until sauce begins to thicken. When the sauce has thickened sufficiently to coat the back of a spoon, remove pot from heat and stir in parsley or mint. To keep sauce warm, use a water bath with hot, but not boiling, water.

Serve sauce next to meat. It is an excellent accompaniment to meat, rice, and any green vegetable you may choose to serve.

Osso Bucco

In 1979 my sister, Susie, and I spent two weeks in Bologna at Marcella Hazan's cooking school where we enjoyed and profited from an in-depth experience of being in Italy with one of the premier Italian chefs. We met food writers, chefs, and restaurateurs, and were introduced to the wonders of extra-virgin olive oil, Parmigiano-Reggiano cheese, and genuine balsamic vinegars. It was a trip to remember.

Yield: 8 servings

8 pieces of veal shank cut into 1½–2-inch pieces
Salt and freshly ground pepper
1 cup flour
8 tablespoons olive oil
3 tablespoons butter
1½ cups chopped onions
¾ cup chopped carrots
¾ cup finely chopped celery
1 large leek (white part only), chopped
1 tablespoon minced garlic
1¼ cups dry white wine
1½ cups good-quality chicken stock
2 pounds ripe tomatoes, peeled, seeded, and chopped, or 1 28-ounce can plum tomatoes, drained and chopped
Large bouquet garni made with parsley, 2 bay leaves, and thyme sprigs

Gremolata

1 tablespoon minced garlic
Rinds of 2 large lemons, finely chopped
½ cup finely chopped parsley

In a small bowl, combine and mix well. Reserve.

Preheat oven to 350 degrees.

Season shanks with salt and pepper. Dredge each piece in flour, shaking off excess. In a large frying pan, heat 3 to 4 tablespoons olive oil. When oil is hot, add half of the shanks, or as many as the pan will hold without crowding, and brown well on all sides. If necessary, add more oil. As each piece is finished, transfer to a plate. Repeat with any remaining shanks.

In a shallow ovenproof casserole large enough to hold all the shanks, melt butter and 3 tablespoons olive oil and sauté onions, carrots, celery, leek, and garlic, stirring frequently until vegetables are lightly colored. At this point, arrange browned veal pieces on top of vegetables.

Pour off any oil left in the frying pan, add wine, and deglaze the pan, scraping the bottom well. When the wine has reduced by half, add the chicken stock and bring to a boil, blending well. Pour liquid over meat and vegetables, scatter the chopped tomatoes on top of the meat, and add the bouquet garni.

Bring the casserole to a full boil on top of the stove. Tuck a piece of foil on top of meat, turning up edges of the foil, and cover. Place in the lower third of the oven and cook 1½ hours or until meat is very tender.

Remove casserole from the oven and transfer pieces of veal to a large plate or platter while making sauce.

Pass liquid and vegetables first through a food mill and then a strainer. Return veal shanks to casserole, pour sauce over meat, and when ready to serve, reheat, covered, for 30 minutes in a preheated 350-degree oven until hot.

To serve: Place a veal shank on each plate, spoon sauce over meat, and finish with a generous sprinkling of gremolata.

Rack of Lamb Persillade

$\mathcal{O}$f all the ways to make rack of lamb, "persillade" is my favorite. This French cooking term describes a mixture of parsley, garlic, and fresh breadcrumbs moistened with olive oil. The crust makes an attractive topping. Pat crumb mixture firmly on top of the racks to make for easier serving.

Yield: 8 servings

2 whole racks of lamb (about 8 chops per rack), trimmed

For best results, have your butcher prepare the racks and give you any trimmings if you plan to make a sauce.

To prepare sauce:

Meat and bone trimmings, cleaned of fat
Butter as needed
½ cup red wine
½ cup port wine
3–4 cups veal or excellent-quality chicken stock
Cornstarch slurry (1 tablespoon cornstarch dissolved in 2 tablespoons cold stock or
    water), optional

Brown meat and bone trimmings in small amount of butter in a frying pan. Turn meat frequently to brown well, being careful not to burn. When trimmings are brown and crisp, blot dry and transfer to a 3-quart saucepot and discard any fat in the frying pan.

Return pan to heat and deglaze with red wine. Add port wine and deglaze again. Add 1 cup stock and reduce liquid to about one-third and transfer to a saucepot. Add 2 more cups of stock, bring to a boil, lower heat, cover, and cook at a simmer for 30 minutes.

Strain stock and remove as much surface fat as possible. Pour into clean frying pan and cook over moderate heat, uncovered, until stock has reduced to a sauce-like consistency.

At this point, a cornstarch slurry may be gradually added to simmering sauce to thicken to desired consistency.

TO PREPARE AND ROAST RACK OF LAMB:

MUSTARD COATING

½ teaspoon salt
Freshly ground pepper
2–3 tablespoons Dijon mustard
3–4 tablespoons olive oil

CRUMB CRUST

1½ cups fresh white breadcrumbs
Enough olive oil to moisten crumbs (about 3–4 tablespoons)
3–4 cloves garlic, minced
4 tablespoons finely chopped parsley

Preheat oven to 500 degrees.

Paint the racks with mustard coating. Set racks, meat side up, in shallow roasting pan in the upper-middle level of the oven. Roast 10 minutes at 500 degrees.

Lower oven to 400 degrees, pat crumb topping evenly over top, and roast approximately 12 to 15 minutes longer.

For a brown topping, place under hot broiler for a few seconds.

Allow meat to rest 10 to 15 minutes before carving.

MOM'S MEAT LOAF

Yield: 6–8 servings

---

1 pound ground chuck
½ pound ground veal
½ pound ground pork
3 slices white bread, ripped into pieces
1 medium onion, grated
2 eggs
½ cup cold water
¼ cup ketchup
Dash Worcestershire sauce
Salt and pepper to taste

Preheat oven to 375 degrees.

Place ground meat in a large bowl.

In the bowl of a food processor, combine bread, grated onion, eggs, water, ketchup, and Worcestershire sauce and process until smooth. Add salt and pepper to taste (about 1 tablespoon salt), process again, then add blended ingredients to meat and mix gently to combine well. Shape mixture into a loaf and place in a shallow baking pan.

Bake 1–1¼ hours.

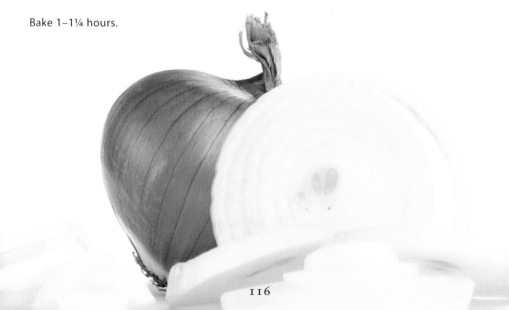

Steak au Poivre

When you are tired of steak, try this easy recipe for Steak au Poivre. Quality filet is readily available, and steaks may be cut to order by the butcher or cut at home. I often demonstrated this recipe in class, and it was well received, especially for Valentine's Day as the perfect romantic dinner.

Yield: 8 servings

4 tablespoons cracked pepper
8 filet steaks, cut into medallions 1-inch thick with excess fat removed
3 tablespoons butter
1 tablespoon vegetable oil
Salt to taste
¼ cup cognac
3 tablespoons finely chopped shallots
2–3 tablespoons green peppercorns, drained
1 cup chicken or veal stock
½ cup heavy cream
¼ cup finely chopped parsley

Crush dried peppercorns in a mortar and pestle, with a rolling pin, or with a meat extender. Firmly press pepper into both sides of steak. Cover with plastic wrap and refrigerate until ready to use.

Melt butter and oil in a large frying pan. Season meat with salt to taste, and when butter-oil mixture is hot, add steaks and sauté over moderately high heat 2 to 3 minutes per side for rare. Heat cognac in a small pot, ignite with a match or from gas burner, and add to meat as it finishes cooking. Remove meat from pan to a side plate. Add shallots to pan and sauté over moderately high heat 1 minute. Add green peppercorns, stock, and cream, and reduce to sauce-like consistency over high heat. Return meat to pan, coat well with sauce, and serve at once. Sprinkle medallions with finely chopped parsley.

Roast Beef with Yorkshire Pudding and Horseradish Cream

Yield: A 6 pound roast yields 8–10 servings

To prepare meat:

Worcestershire sauce, about a couple tablespoons
1 large onion, sliced
2-3 cloves garlic, sliced into thin slivers
Salt and pepper to taste

Rub the rib roast with Worcestershire sauce. Attach onion slices to top of roast with toothpicks. Insert garlic slivers between meat and fat on the roast. Season liberally with salt and pepper.

Rib roast, like all large pieces of meat, should stand at least one hour at room temperature before roasting.

Time can only be approximate, since the size and shape of the roast, the amount of bone, and the proportions of lean and fat affect cooking time. An instant-read meat thermometer inserted in the fleshy part of the roast, and not touching the bone, ensures accuracy. A temperature of 120 degrees indicates rare.

Sear the roast in a hot oven (500 degrees) 10 to 15 minutes. Reduce heat to moderate (325 to 350 degrees; 325 degrees is preferred for larger roast) for the remainder of the cooking time. Including the time the meat is seared, allow 18 to 20 minutes per pound for rare, 22 to 25 for medium, and 27 minutes for well done.

While the roast is cooking, prepare the batter for the yorkshire pudding and horseradish cream.

Yorkshire Pudding

Yield: 8 servings

1½ cups flour
1 teaspoon salt
¾ cup milk
¾ cup water
3 eggs

Place flour and salt in a food processor, using the metal blade. Add milk and water and process until smooth. With spatula, scrape down sides. Add eggs one at a time, blending after each addition, to make a creamy batter. Pour batter into a bowl or jar, cover, and let rest 2 hours.

When the roast is done, remove from oven. Raise oven temperature to 450 degrees. Spoon 6 tablespoons drippings (enough to lightly coat bottom of pan) into a shallow baking pan and set in the oven to become sizzling hot. Beat, or shake, the batter vigorously and pour into hot pan. Bake 15 minutes, and when pudding has puffed and lightly browned, reduce temperature to 350 degrees and bake 15 minutes longer, or until pudding is light, crisp, and brown. Cut into squares.

Horseradish Cream

---

1 cup heavy cream
1 jar (4 ounces) prepared white horseradish, drained
Dash sugar
Salt and freshly ground pepper to taste

Whip cream slightly. Mix in drained horseradish and season. Refrigerate until serving time.

Carve roast and serve with yorkshire pudding and horseradish cream on the side.

Veal Scallops Parmesan

In the early days of my marriage, veal was very popular and the centerpiece of many dinner parties. Today, that is no longer the case, but I cannot resist including this wonderful veal recipe. Veal Scallops Parmesan was the favorite birthday dinner for our middle son, Alan. And I must confess, every so often, I enjoy making and serving this dish today.

Yield: 6–8 servings

1 pound veal, cut into scallops
Salt and freshly ground pepper
Flour for dredging
2 eggs
2 teaspoons water
1½ cups dried breadcrumbs, mixed with 2 teaspoons dried Italian herbs
    and ¼ cup grated Parmigiano-Reggiano or other Parmesan cheese
Olive oil and vegetable oil for frying (enough to come ½ inch up pan)

Flatten veal slices with a meat pounder (one without spikes) to approximately ⅓ inch thick. Season lightly with salt and pepper and dredge slices in flour, shaking off excess.

Beat eggs with water. Dip floured veal pieces into mixture and then into seasoned crumbs. Arrange veal in a single layer on a plate covered with a sheet of waxed paper. Heat oils in a frying pan and, when hot, sauté veal pieces until golden brown on both sides. Drain on paper toweling and salt lightly. Reserve.

Sauce

½ cup dry red or white wine
2 cups tomato sauce
½ teaspoon oregano or other dried Italian herb
1 tablespoon minced parsley
Dash sugar
Salt and pepper

Drain oil from frying pan and deglaze with wine, scraping brown bits from bottom and sides of pan. Add remaining ingredients. Mix well. Bring to a boil and simmer, covered, about 15 minutes.

To assemble veal:

Sauce
Cooked veal pieces
½ pound mozzarella cheese, sliced thin
¼–⅓ pound Fontina cheese, coarsely grated
Freshly grated Parmigiano-Reggiano or other Parmesan cheese

Preheat oven to 375 degrees.

Spread about ⅓ cup sauce or enough to cover the bottom. In gratin dish or shallow baking dish, arrange veal slices overlapping with slices of mozzarella cheese in between. Nap with another third of the sauce. Scatter coarsely grated Fontina cheese over top. Drizzle remaining sauce over veal and top with grated Parmesan cheese.

Heat in oven until sauce is hot and cheese is melted.

BREADS AND MUFFINS

Banana Nut Muffins
124

Favorite Blueberry Muffins
125

Rich Baking Powder Biscuits
125

Scones
126

Sour Cream Coffee Cake
127

Kalamata Sun-Dried Tomato
Cheese Bread
128

Parmesan Cheese Bread
129

Banana Nut Muffins

The perfect way to use up overripe or extra bananas is to make a batch of Banana Nut Muffins. Walnuts and bananas pair beautifully, and if you keep a batch of muffins in the freezer, you can make a hurry-up ordinary breakfast a special occasion.

Yield: 18 muffins

---

1 extra-large egg
1½ cups milk
6 tablespoons (¾ stick) butter, melted and slightly cooled
3 cups sifted all-purpose flour
6 tablespoons sugar
1 tablespoon plus ½ teaspoon baking powder
1½ teaspoons salt
1½ cups mashed very ripe bananas (3–4)
½ cup chopped, lightly toasted walnuts

Preheat oven to 400 degrees. Grease muffin tin.

Beat egg lightly with a fork. Stir in milk and melted butter. Sift together flour, sugar, baking powder, and salt and add to egg mixture, stirring only until flour is moistened and batter is blended. Add mashed banana and walnuts and mix only until blended.

Divide batter among 18 muffin cups, filling almost to the top, and bake 20 to 25 minute

Between the lines: Nuts are usually harvested once a year, in the fall. When buying nuts, buy in the fall and store them in the freezer. When buying out of season, it is best to buy vacuum-sealed product.

Favorite Blueberry Muffins

Yield: 12 muffins

¼ cup butter
¼ cup sugar
1 egg
2 cups all-purpose flour
4 teaspoons baking powder
½ teaspoon salt
1 cup milk
1½ cups fresh blueberries

Preheat oven to 375 degrees. Grease muffin tin.

In the bowl of an electric mixer, soften butter with beater and gradually add sugar, creaming well. Add egg and beat again. Sift flour with baking powder and salt. Add dry ingredients to first mixture alternately with milk, beating after each addition. Fold blueberries gently into batter and fill muffin cups three-fourths full. Bake 25 to 30 minutes, or until lightly browned.

Rich Baking Powder Biscuits

Yield: One 9-inch round cake pan of biscuits

---

2 cups sifted all-purpose unbleached flour
1 teaspoon salt
1 tablespoon baking powder
¼ teaspoon sugar
1 cup heavy cream
4 tablespoons butter, melted

Preheat oven to 425 degrees.

Sift dry ingredients together. Quickly fold in heavy cream with large rubber spatula. If absolutely necessary, add a small amount of additional cream to hold dough together.

continued

Turn onto a lightly floured board, knead no more than 1 minute, then pat or gently roll into a dough ½-inch thick. With a biscuit cutter, cut into rounds.

Coat the bottom of a 9-inch round cake pan with 3 tablespoons of the melted butter. Place biscuits in the pan and brush tops with remaining butter. Bake 12 to 15 minutes, or until tops are golden brown.

Scones

*T*hese tender, tasty breakfast biscuits are delicious with your favorite jam or preserves. For a tender crumb, do not overwork the dough.

Yield: Approximately 12 scones

---

2 cups all-purpose flour
4 teaspoons granulated sugar
1 tablespoon baking powder
⅛ teaspoon baking soda
½ teaspoon salt
⅔ cup cold unsalted butter
¼ cup currants, or more to taste, softened in boiling water 1 minute, then drained
⅔ cup buttermilk
1 egg, beaten with 1 tablespoon milk

Preheat oven to 400 degrees. Lightly grease a baking sheet.

Combine flour, sugar, baking powder, baking soda, and salt in a mixing bowl. Cut in cold butter until mixture forms coarse crumbs. Mix in currants, then make a well in the center of the mixture and add buttermilk, mixing with a fork until mixture clings together. Turn onto a floured board and knead lightly until dough is smooth. Do not overwork.

Lightly roll dough 1 to 1¼ inches thick and form scones with a 2-inch round cutter. Place 2 inches apart on prepared baking sheet. Brush tops with beaten egg and milk and bake 15 minutes, or until golden brown. Serve warm with preserves.

Sour Cream Coffee Cake

Yield: 12 servings

½ cup butter
1 cup sugar
2 eggs, lightly beaten
1 teaspoon baking powder
¼ teaspoon salt
1 teaspoon baking soda
2 cups all-purpose flour, unsifted
1 cup sour cream

Preheat oven to 350 degrees. Butter a 9x13-inch pan.

Cream butter and sugar until light. Add eggs and blend. Combine baking powder, salt, baking soda, and flour, and add alternately with sour cream, blending after each addition. Pour into prepared pan.

Topping:

---

1 cup brown sugar
2 teaspoons cinnamon
½ cup chopped pecans
¼ cup flour
¼ cup butter

In a bowl, combine brown sugar, cinnamon, nuts, flour, and butter, and with a pastry blender or two knives, cut mixture into small pieces. Sprinkle over top of batter and bake for 30 minutes, or until a toothpick inserted in the center comes out clean.

Kalamata Sun-Dried Tomato Cheese Bread

Yield: Two braided loaves, approximately 1½ pounds each

2 packages active dry yeast (4½ teaspoons)
½ cup warm water
1¼ cups warm milk
2 tablespoons honey
1 egg, beaten
2 teaspoons salt
1 cup pitted and coarsely chopped Kalamata olives
½ cup coarsely chopped sun-dried tomatoes, softened in hot water
½ cup finely chopped flat-leaf parsley
5½–6½ cups unbleached all-purpose flour
8 ounces feta cheese, coarsely grated or crumbled
Egg wash (1 egg, beaten with 1 tablespoon milk or cold water)

In the large bowl of an electric mixer, soften the yeast in the warm water. Incorporate the milk, honey, egg, salt, olives, tomatoes, parsley, and 2 cups of the flour, then beat at medium-high speed for 2 minutes. Gradually add as much of the remaining flour required to form a mass of dough that begins to pull away from the sides of the bowl. Turn the dough onto a floured surface and knead, adding more flour as needed, until dough is smooth and elastic.

Place dough in oiled bowl, turn to coat the entire ball of dough, cover bowl with plastic wrap, and let dough rise in a warm place until doubled in size, about 1 hour.

Divide dough in half and place one half on a floured work surface and flatten or roll into a 15-inch square. Sprinkle with feta cheese. Roll the dough towards you to form a cylinder. Cover and allow dough to rest 10 minutes. Repeat with second piece of dough.

To make a braid: Cut the first dough cylinder into three equal pieces. With the palm of your hands, roll each piece into a 15- to 20-inch rope. Lay the ropes side by side. Starting in the center, braid the dough. Turn the dough and braid the other end. Coil the bread and tuck the end under to keep it from unwinding. Use a second baking sheet for second loaf. Place on greased baking sheet, cover, and let rise for 45 minutes.

Preheat oven to 375 degrees. Brush top and sides with egg wash and bake for 30 to 35 minutes, or until bread is golden brown and sounds hollow when tapped.

Remove from oven and cool on a rack.

Parmesan Cheese Bread

Yield: One 8-inch round loaf

---

1 package (2¼ teaspoons) active dry yeast
¼ cup warm water
1½ cups unbleached all-purpose flour
1 tablespoon sugar
½ teaspoon salt
⅓ cup butter
1 egg, beaten
¼ cup milk, at room temperature
½ cup grated Parmesan cheese
¼ cup minced parsley
Egg glaze (1 egg yolk beaten with 1 tablespoon milk, cream, or water)

Preheat oven to 350 degrees. Butter 8-inch round cake pan.

Dissolve yeast in warm water 5 minutes, or until foamy.

Place flour, sugar, and salt in the bowl of an electric mixer. Using a pastry blender or two knives, cut butter into dry ingredients to resemble coarse meal. Add egg, dissolved yeast, and milk, and beat 1 minute at low speed to combine ingredients. Add grated cheese and parsley. Turn mixer to high and beat 1 to 2 minutes, until dough shreds from beaters and pulls away from the side of the bowl. Gather into a dough, knead a few minutes to form a smooth and elastic dough, then turn into prepared pan.

Cover dough loosely with plastic wrap and allow to rise 50 to 60 minutes, until doubled.

Bake 20 to 25 minutes. Remove from oven and brush top of bread with egg glaze. Bake 15 minutes more. Cool on a rack before removing from pan.

DESSERTS

PIES

PIE PASTRY
132

UPSIDE-DOWN APPLE PIE
133

ANCHO CHILE FUDGE PIE
134

APPLE ASIAGO PIE
136

BANANA CREAM PIE
137

MY MOTHER'S COCONUT CREAM PIE
138

HONEY AND CHEESE PIE
139

SUMMER FRUIT CROSTATA
140

Pie Pastry

My mother loved to make pies, and as a child, I enjoyed watching her measure flour, salt, and shortening into a mixing bowl. Using a pastry blender, she rapidly blended the ingredients and stopped when the mixture resembled peas. The final step was to gradually add tablespoons of ice water, stopping when the dough was malleable. By this time, my younger sister, Susie, usually joined us. I think what both of us girls liked best was when, after rolling out the crust, she made small pies by rolling the scraps into thin rounds, brushing them with butter, and sprinkling a mix of sugar and cinnamon over the top. When I was a mother, my three boys sustained the family tradition. They loved these "pies" and took pride in making their own Stanley, Alan, and Rodger "specials."

Yield: One double-crust pie shell or two single-crust pie shells

---

2 cups sifted unbleached all-purpose flour
1 teaspoon salt
⅔ cup chilled shortening (Crisco preferred)
5–7 tablespoons ice water

Mix together flour and salt. Cut in shortening with pastry blender until the largest pieces are the size of peas. Sprinkle 1 tablespoon water over part of mixture. Gently toss with fork; push to one side of the bowl. Sprinkle second tablespoon of water over dry part, mix lightly, and push to moistened part at side. Repeat until all flour is moistened. Form dough into a ball and divide into two pieces.

On lightly floured surface, flatten each piece of dough with rolling pin, smoothing edges. Roll to ⅛ inch thick. Roll from the center, using light strokes. For single crust, fold in half, then in half again, and unfold over pie plate, fitting loosely onto bottom and sides. Trim pastry ½ inch beyond rim, fold under, and form an edge by using fingers or fork. For double crust, follow specific recipe.

Between the lines: When making a crust, do not overwork ingredients. It is easier to use cold shortening (I keep Crisco in the refrigerator) and ice water.

Use a pastry blender or two knives to cut in the shortening. Fingers give off heat and break down the shortening. It is not necessary to chill this dough, and you may use it right away. When rolling out the dough, roll away from you on a right angle. Using a pastry cloth allows you to move the dough without touching it. Remember, overworking the dough tends to toughen it.

Upside-Down Apple Pie

In Pittsburgh, Stouffer's restaurant was a popular choice for lunch or dinner downtown. My father, an ophthalmologist, had his office in the Jenkins Arcade, diagonally across the street from Stouffer's. I loved to go there for lunch with my mother, and later on, with girlfriends. My favorite dishes were spinach soufflé, cheese rarebit, macaroni and cheese, and almost any kind of pie or cake. Upside-Down Apple Pie was one of the best.

Yield: One double-crust 9-inch pie

1 recipe Pie Pastry (p. 132)
⅓ cup firmly packed brown sugar
4 tablespoons (½ stick) butter, melted
¼ cup chopped walnuts or pecans
3½ cups peeled apples, cut into sixths
½ cup granulated sugar
2 tablespoons flour
½ teaspoon cinnamon
Dash nutmeg
Dash salt

Prepare pie pastry, but do not put bottom crust in pie plate yet.

Sprinkle brown sugar over bottom of pie plate. Pour melted butter over brown sugar to combine. Sprinkle nuts over mixture. Carefully place pastry for bottom crust on top of nuts. Trim crust even with edge of pan. Fill with apples.

continued

Mix granulated sugar, flour, cinnamon, nutmeg, and salt and sprinkle over apples. Place pastry for top crust over apples. Trim even with pan. Press top and bottom crusts together, turning under and away from pan edge. Prick top crust 4 or 5 times with a fork.

Place on a cookie sheet and bake 45 to 60 minutes, or until crust is golden brown. Remove pie from pan immediately. Run spatula around edge to loosen, hold plate over pie, and invert. Allow sugar mixture to drip onto pie from pan before removing pie plate.

Ancho Chile Fudge Pie

*C*hef Larry Bowen worked at the old Westin William Penn Hotel for an all too short time. His heart belonged to Texas, and after a brief stay, Westin transferred him back to Houston. His farewell recipe for my "À la Carte" *Pittsburgh Press* column was this wonderful Southwestern pie. Chocolate and chile play well off each other to create a subtle rich and spicy taste.

Yield: 8–10 servings

½ recipe Pie Pastry (p. 132)
½ pound (2 sticks) unsalted butter
6 ounces semisweet chocolate, cut into small pieces, or 1 cup chocolate chips
2 eggs
½ cup granulated sugar
½ cup light brown sugar
½ cup plus 2 tablespoons all-purpose flour
2 tablespoons Ancho Chile Puree (see p. 135)
½ cup lightly toasted chopped pecans
½ cup lightly toasted chopped walnuts
1 tablespoon vanilla
1 cup heavy cream, whipped, for garnish

Prepare pie pastry. It is not necessary to prick the bottom or sides of the crust. Simply trim edge ½ inch beyond rim and fold under. Flute edge with fingers or fork tines. Crust is now ready to use.

Melt butter and chocolate together and let cool.

Preheat oven to 400 degrees. In bowl of an electric mixer, beat eggs until foamy, add sugars gradually, and beat until well blended. Blend in cooled chocolate and butter mixture. On low speed, add flour and Ancho Chile Puree, and mix until smooth. Stir in nuts and vanilla. Pour filling into pie shell and bake 40 to 45 minutes, until filling is set. Serve warm or at room temperature with dollop of whipped cream.

To make Ancho Chile Puree: Drop 4 or 5 large ancho chiles in boiling water (off the heat) and weight them with a heavy lid or plate. Steep 20 minutes. Remove chiles, stem and seed them, and remove skins. Mash pulp with a fork or puree in processor or blender until smooth, thinning with a few tablespoons of soaking liquid if necessary. Keep refrigerated in a tightly closed jar, or for longer keeping, freeze.

Apple Asiago Pie

Yield: 8–10 servings

½ recipe Pie Pastry (p. 132)

Prepare pie pastry, place in pie plate, and form rim.

Apple Filling

½ cup granulated sugar (2 plus tablespoons more if apples are very tart)
1 teaspoon cinnamon
2 tablespoons flour
Dash nutmeg
3–4 grindings pepper
6–7 Golden Delicious, Granny Smith, or other pie apples, peeled, cored, and cut into slices

Mix granulated sugar, cinnamon, flour, nutmeg, and pepper in a large bowl and combine with sliced apples. Turn filling into pie shell.

Cheese Crumb Topping

6 tablespoons (¾ stick) cold unsalted butter, cut into pieces
½ cup packed light brown sugar
¾ cup all-purpose flour
3 ounces Asiago cheese, grated or cut into small dice

Place all ingredients but cheese in a bowl and, using a pastry blender, blend until crumbly. Mix in cheese and sprinkle over apples.

Preheat oven to 400 degrees.

Place pie on a cookie sheet and bake 55 to 60 minutes, or until topping is brown and apples are bubbling.

Banana Cream Pie

Yield: 8–10 servings

¾ cup sugar

3 tablespoons cornstarch

¼ teaspoon salt

2 cups milk

3 egg yolks, slightly beaten

1 tablespoon butter

2 teaspoons vanilla, divided

2–3 bananas

½ recipe Pie Pastry (p. 132), baked

1 cup heavy cream

In a saucepan, combine sugar, cornstarch, and salt; gradually stir in milk. Cook and stir over medium heat until mixture boils. Cook 2 minutes longer; remove from heat and stir a small amount of the mixture into yolks. Return to hot mixture and cook, stirring, 2 minutes. Remove from heat. Add butter and 1 teaspoon of the vanilla. Cool to room temperature.

Cut bananas into thin slices to cover the bottom of the pie in two layers. Top with cooled custard filling. Add remaining teaspoon of vanilla to cream and whip until stiff. Do not overbeat. Spread whipped cream evenly over top. Refrigerate. Allow pie to sit at room temperature 30 minutes before serving.

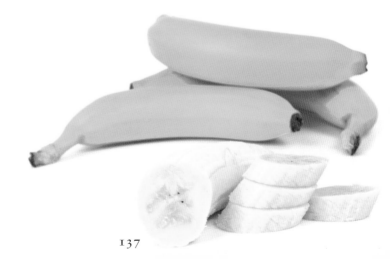

My Mother's Coconut Cream Pie

My mother loved Coconut Cream Pie, and she made a good one. Here is her recipe. I think you will like it.

Yield: 8 servings

¼ cup cornstarch
⅔ cup granulated sugar
¼ teaspoon salt
2 cups milk
3 egg yolks, slightly beaten
2 tablespoons butter
1 teaspoon vanilla, divided
1½ cups fresh or moist shredded coconut, divided
½ recipe Pie Pastry (p. 132), baked
1¼ cups heavy cream

Combine cornstarch, sugar, and salt in a medium-sized heavy-bottomed pot. Gradually add milk, stirring to combine. Cook over medium heat, stirring constantly, until mixture thickens and boils. Cook 2 minutes more, then remove from heat. Add small amount to egg yolks and stir back into milk mixture. Cook 1 minute, at a strong simmer, stirring constantly. Add butter, ½ teaspoon of the vanilla, and 1 cup of the coconut. Cool to room temperature and pour into baked pastry shell. While pie is cooling, whip cream with remaining ½ teaspoon vanilla, until stiff but not dry. Cover pie with whipped cream, sprinkle with remaining ½ cup coconut, and refrigerate until ready to serve.

Between the lines: If desired, lightly toast the ½ cup coconut to be sprinkled over whipped cream. Be careful—coconut burns easily and quickly.

Honey and Cheese Pie

A favorite pie from my travels to Mykonos and discovery of good things Greek.

Yield: 8 generous or 10 small servings

½ recipe Pie Pastry (p. 132)

Filling

1 cup (4–5 ounces) dried apricots
1 pound ricotta cheese
½ cup honey
4 large eggs
1 tablespoon lemon juice
Grated rind of 1 lemon
½ cup heavy cream
1 tablespoon flour

Preheat oven to 400 degrees. Place dried apricots in a small pan. Cover with water, bring to a boil, lower heat, and simmer 5 minutes. Drain and cut apricots into small pieces. Set aside.

Combine cheese and honey in the bowl of an electric mixer. Add eggs one at a time, beating well after each addition. Add lemon juice, rind, and heavy cream and blend well. Toss apricots with flour, coating evenly, then fold into filling. Pour filling into unbaked pie crust and bake 45 to 50 minutes, until filling is set and crust lightly browned.

Glaze

¼ cup strained apricot jam
1 tablespoon Grand Marnier or other orange-flavored liqueur

Combine apricot jam and Grand Marnier in small pan and heat until mixture boils. Brush or spread glaze over top of pie.

Summer Fruit Crostata

*O*ne of the best cooking demos I have seen was taught in tandem by Margrit Mondavi and her daughter, Annie Roberts. Mrs. Mondavi conducted a dialogue with her daughter and the audience, and she shared many personal and cooking anecdotes from her long history at the Robert Mondavi Winery in Napa Valley. To me, a cooking class has succeeded if I go home and make one or two of the recipes. When class was over, I stopped at the grocery store, and that night we enjoyed Annie Roberts' Raspberry Crostata for dessert.

Yield: 8 servings (1 small crostata)

½ recipe (10 ounces) Short Butter Pastry (p. 141)
3–4 tablespoons granulated sugar, divided
2–3 cups fresh raspberries, or other fruit
1 tablespoon butter, cut into small pieces
Confectioners' sugar
Crème fraîche, whipped cream, or vanilla ice cream (optional)

Preheat oven to 450 degrees.

Roll out dough on lightly floured surface to form an 11-inch circle. Transfer to baking sheet and sprinkle with 1 tablespoon of the sugar. Allowing a 1½ inch border, cover the dough with raspberries, stem side down in a single layer. If there are extra berries, mound in the center. Sprinkle berries with most of the remaining sugar, reserving a small amount to sprinkle over crust. Dot fruit with butter pieces.

Turn up dough border to enclose the sides of the tart and to cover some of the fruit. Press down dough on the baking sheet, securing sides and bottom of the pastry, but do not mash any fruit. Gently pinch soft pleats in the pastry border and sprinkle it with reserved sugar.

Bake the tart 20 to 25 minutes, until the fruit has given off some of its juice and the crust is golden.

Cool on rack for 10 minutes. Dust with confectioners sugar and serve warm or at room temperature, garnishing with crème fraîche, whipped cream, or a scoop of vanilla ice cream, if desired.

Short Butter Pastry

Yield: Approximately 20 ounces of dough, enough for one large or two small crostatas

---

½ pound (2 sticks) unsalted butter, cut into ½-inch cubes
2 cups unbleached all-purpose flour
¼ cup granulated sugar
1 teaspoon salt
¼ cup ice water

While assembling ingredients place butter cubes in the freezer for 10 minutes.

Place flour, sugar, and salt in the container of a food processor. Using the steel blade, pulse one or two times to combine dry ingredients.

Add butter and pulse 15 to 18 times, or until butter particles are the size of peas. Do not overwork dough.

With the motor running, add the water all at once, stopping the machine before the dough forms a mass. The mixture will be very loose. Turn out onto a floured board and gather loose pieces into one large or two smaller disks. Wrap in wax paper and place in the drawer of the refrigerator for one hour.

When ready to roll out dough, allow dough to soften at room temperature 10 to 15 minutes first.

CAKES

AUNT SUSIE'S FESTIVE BLITZ TORTE
143

FRESH COCONUT CAKE
145

HAZELNUT TORTE
147

HOMEMADE ICE CREAM ROLL
149

MOCHA RUM WHIPPED CREAM ROLL
150

MY MOTHER'S BUTTERMILK CAKE
152

PINEAPPLE UPSIDE-DOWN CAKE
153

SACHERTORTE
155

TARTE AU FROMAGE
157

AUNT SUSIE'S FESTIVE BLITZ TORTE

*favorite of my sister Susie's, the original recipe came from *Cake Secrets*, a small paperback cookbook offered by Swans Down Flour for a box top and a nominal amount of money. The cookbook was a favorite of my mother's, and I used my only copy until it fell apart.

Yield: 10–12 servings

1¾ cups sifted cake flour
2¼ teaspoons baking powder
¾ teaspoon salt
2 cups plus 2 tablespoons granulated sugar
4 egg whites, unbeaten
¼ pound (1 stick) unsalted butter, at room temperature
⅔ cup minus 1 tablespoon milk
2 teaspoons vanilla, divided
2 whole eggs, unbeaten
½ cup slivered blanched almonds
Pineapple Filling
1 cup heavy cream

Use two 9-inch round cake pans, 1½ inches deep. Butter and line bottoms with wax paper. Preheat oven to 350 degrees.

Measure sifted flour into sifter; add baking powder, salt, and 1 cup plus 2 tablespoons of the sugar and reserve.

Beat egg whites until foamy. Gradually add remaining cup of sugar and beat to stiff peaks.

In the large bowl of an electric mixer, stir butter to soften. Sift in dry ingredients. Add milk and 1 teaspoon of the vanilla. Mix until flour is dampened, then beat 2 minutes on low speed. Add 2 eggs and beat 1 minute longer.

continued

Pour batter into pans. Spread beaten egg whites over batter and sprinkle with almonds. Bake 35 to 40 minutes, or until meringue is lightly browned and cake pulls away from sides of pan. Cool on racks.

Loosen sides of cooled cake with metal spatula. Invert pan and place one layer on plate with meringue side down. Spread Pineapple Filling evenly over top and place second layer on filling, using meringue as top of cake. Combine heavy cream and remaining 1 teaspoon vanilla and whip until stiff. Spread whipped cream evenly around sides of cake.

Pineapple Filling

¼ cup sugar
1 tablespoon flour
Dash salt
⅔ cup milk
2 egg yolks, lightly beaten
1 tablespoon butter
1 small can crushed pineapple, drained

Combine sugar, flour, and salt in a heavy saucepan. Mix milk with egg yolks and add to mixture. Cook over low heat, stirring, until thickened. Remove from heat. Add butter and drained fruit, then mix. Cool before using to fill cake.

Fresh Coconut Cake

Fresh Coconut Cake is truly a festive, special occasion cake. When I was growing up, Joyce-McClements in East Liberty and the Waldorf Bakery in Squirrel Hill were famous for their delicious coconut cakes. I make my own version using a sponge cake. Though there are several steps involved, the recipe is not difficult and is well worth the effort.

Yield: 16 servings

To prepare coconut:

1 fresh coconut (when buying, shake and be sure coconut is not dry; you should hear the coconut milk moving inside)

Pierce three holes at one end of the coconut. Drain the milk and discard. Place coconut on baking sheet and heat in 350-degree oven for 30 minutes. Cool. Break shell with a hammer, remove meat, and break meat into pieces. With a vegetable peeler, remove the brown skin. Grate or shred the coconut meat by hand or in a food processor. Wrap in plastic wrap or put in a ziplock bag and store in the refrigerator. Grated coconut may also be frozen.

To prepare cake:

1½ cups sifted all-purpose flour
1½ cups granulated sugar, divided
½ cup egg yolks (8)
¼ cup cold water
1 tablespoon lemon juice
1 teaspoon vanilla
1 cup egg whites (12)
1 teaspoon cream of tartar
1 teaspoon salt

Preheat oven to 350 degrees.

continued

Sift flour and ¾ cup of the sugar into a large mixing bowl. Make a well in the center; add egg yolks, water, lemon juice, and vanilla. Beat until smooth.

Beat egg whites with cream of tartar and salt just until soft peaks form; add remaining ¾ cup sugar gradually (about 2 tablespoons at a time) and continue to beat until stiff. Gently fold egg whites into first mixture.

Pour batter into ungreased 10-inch tube pan. Carefully cut through batter with a metal spatula to break air bubbles. Bake 45 to 50 minutes, or until top springs back when lightly touched. Invert pan 1 hour or until cool. Remove cake. Split horizontally into four equal layers. Assemble cake with Custard Cream Filling and frost with whipped cream.

Whipped Cream

2 cups heavy cream
2 teaspoons vanilla

Place heavy cream in mixing bowl and add 2 teaspoons vanilla. With an electric mixer or balloon whisk, beat cream until stiff. Reserve and refrigerate two-thirds of the whipped cream for frosting the cake and use the other one-third for the Custard Cream Filling.

Custard Cream Filling

1 cup milk
½ cup granulated sugar
¼ teaspoon salt
2 tablespoons cornstarch
1 egg
1 tablespoon butter
½ teaspoon vanilla
Reserved ⅓ of the whipped cream

Heat milk in a small saucepan until it boils.

Combine sugar, salt, cornstarch, and egg in a heavy saucepan and gradually stir in the milk.

Cook over moderate heat, stirring constantly, until mixture thickens. Remove from heat, add butter and vanilla, and stir until butter melts. Cool. Fold in the reserved one-third of the whipped cream into the custard.

To assemble cake: After cake is cut into four layers, arrange bottom layer on cake plate and spread generously with Custard Cream Filling, spreading right to the edges. Repeat with the second and third layers. Place fourth layer on top and frost the top and sides of the cake generously with the reserved two-thirds of the whipped cream. Cover generously with grated coconut.

Between the lines: I recommend making the cake a few days ahead and storing in the freezer wrapped in foil. I use a serrated bread knife to cut the cake, and recommend slicing the layers before the cake has fully defrosted.

HAZELNUT TORTE

*B*etween the ages of eight and eleven, I spent the summers with my family outside Atlantic City, New Jersey. In Ventnor, my mother would shop at the Swiss Pastry Shop, a European bakery that made the most delicious hazelnut cake. I never forgot it, and early in my marriage, I came up with a reasonable copy which I would make every Thanksgiving for dessert.

Yield: 12 or more servings

9 eggs, separated
⅔ cup granulated sugar, divided
1 teaspoon vanilla
1 cup lightly toasted and finely ground hazelnuts
⅔ cup sifted all-purpose flour
1–2 tablespoons water, if needed
¼ teaspoon salt
Flavored whipped cream
2–3 ounces bittersweet chocolate, shaved or coarsely grated

Preheat oven to 325 degrees. Butter and flour three 9-inch round cake pans.

continued

Place yolks in mixing bowl and gradually add ⅓ cup of the sugar, beating until light. With a rubber spatula, fold in vanilla, hazelnuts, and sifted flour, blending lightly but well. If mixture seems too dry, add 1 to 2 tablespoons water and blend.

Beat the 9 egg whites with the salt until foamy. Gradually add the remaining ⅓ cup sugar, beating until whites are stiff but not dry. Beat one-fourth of the egg whites into the batter and gradually fold in the rest.

Divide among prepared pans and bake in the center of oven for 15 to 20 minutes, or until cake shrinks from sides of pan and springs back when touched in the center. Cool 10 minutes and turn out onto racks to completely cool.

TO MAKE FLAVORED WHIPPED CREAM:

2½ cups heavy cream
3 tablespoons sifted unsweetened cocoa
2 teaspoons powdered instant coffee
1 teaspoon vanilla
3–4 tablespoons confectioners' sugar

Combine heavy cream, cocoa, instant coffee, vanilla, and confectioners' sugar in the bowl of an electric mixer. Whip until cream holds soft peaks. Do not overbeat. Spread between cooled cake layers and frost the top and sides. Garnish with chocolate.

Homemade Ice Cream Roll

This recipe was my mother's, and a family favorite when I was growing up. It remained a favorite with my husband and children, who still enjoy the dessert today. It is a great dessert to have on hand in the freezer. The cake is versatile, and though vanilla ice cream is traditional, any ice cream can be used. For example, try butter pecan with warm caramel sauce, mint chocolate chip with warm chocolate sauce, or black raspberry ice cream with fresh peaches.

Yield: 10–12 small slices

Confectioners' sugar
4 eggs (graded large or extra-large), at room temperature
¾ teaspoon baking powder
½ teaspoon salt
¾ cup granulated sugar
1 teaspoon vanilla extract
¾ cup sifted cake flour
½ gallon (or less) ice cream, softened
Caramel Sauce (optional)

Preheat oven to 350 degrees. Grease and flour a 15x10x1-inch nonstick jelly-roll pan.

Sprinkle confectioners' sugar over a clean cotton or linen dishtowel.

Place eggs, baking powder, and salt in the bowl of an electric mixer. Beat at high speed for 3 minutes, or until thick and lemon-colored. Reduce speed slightly and gradually add the granulated sugar. Increase speed and beat until mixture is very thick and falls in a heavy ribbon when beaters are raised. Beat in vanilla, then sift the flour over batter and incorporate flour by folding or at low speed. Do not overbeat.

Spread batter evenly in pan and bake 12 to 15 minutes, until top springs back when lightly touched and sides shrink from pan. Do not overbake. Remove from oven and immediately turn out onto a towel sprinkled with confectioners' sugar. Roll lengthwise with towel and cool. Unroll and spread with softened ice cream. Roll up, wrap in foil, and freeze. Serve with Caramel Sauce, if desired.

continued

Between the lines: It is very important not to overbake the cake, or it will crack when you try to roll it. I work with a half gallon of ice cream but never use it all (unless I succumb to the temptation of digging in with a spoon!).

CARAMEL SAUCE

Yield: Approximately 1 cup

---

1 cup granulated sugar
½ cup water
Few drops of lemon juice
1 cup heavy cream

Combine the sugar and water in a heavy saucepan and cook over moderate heat. A few drops of lemon juice added to water will help stop any crystallization. If sugar does begin to crystallize around the edges of the pan, brush down with cold water. Do not stir, and be careful that sugar does not burn.

When contents of pan turn amber brown, remove from the heat and immediately add the cream, stirring until smooth. Return sauce to heat and cook 5 minutes or so over moderate heat, until sauce has thickened slightly.

MOCHA RUM WHIPPED CREAM ROLL

Yield: 10–12 small slices

---

4 large eggs, separated
⅔ cup granulated sugar, divided
⅓ cup sifted cake flour
1 teaspoon baking powder
¼ teaspoon salt
¼ cup unsweetened cocoa (Droste preferred)
1 tablespoon instant coffee, dissolved in 3 tablespoons hot water
⅓ cup ground almonds
Dash of salt
Whipped Cream Filling

Preheat oven to 350 degrees. Grease and flour a 15x10x1-inch nonstick jelly-roll pan. Sprinkle an open dishtowel with an even layer of cocoa passed through a strainer.

Place egg yolks in the bowl of an electric mixer and beat at medium speed for 3 minutes, until thick. Gradually add ⅓ cup of the sugar, beating until light and lemon-colored.

Sift cake flour, baking powder, salt, and cocoa together and, on low speed, add to egg yolks alternately with coffee, mixing well. Fold in ground almonds. (If mixture seems overly thick, thin with 1 to 2 tablespoons hot water.)

Place egg whites in a large mixing bowl and beat on medium speed until foamy. Add salt, turn mixer on high, and beat until soft peaks form. Gradually add remaining ⅓ cup sugar, beating until whites are stiff but not dry. Beat in one-fourth of the beaten whites to lighten batter, and then fold in remaining whites. Spread batter evenly in prepared pan.

Bake 12 minutes, or until cake springs back to the touch and pulls away from pan. Immediately turn out onto cocoa dusted towel, loosening sides with a spatula first. Roll cake and towel together tightly, starting on the long side closest to you. Place seam side down to cool completely before filling.

WHIPPED CREAM FILLING

2 cups heavy cream
3 tablespoons confectioners' sugar
1 teaspoon vanilla
2–3 tablespoons dark rum

Place heavy cream, confectioners' sugar, vanilla, and rum in a large mixing bowl and mix to combine. Chill 15 minutes before beating. While cream is chilling, make a stabilizer for the cream:

1½ tablespoons cold water
¾ teaspoon unflavored gelatin

continued

Put water in a small custard dish. Sprinkle gelatin over the water and allow to stand 5 minutes. Set the dish into a small pan filled with ½ inch of hot water. Heat, stirring constantly, until gelatin is completely dissolved. Cool slightly but do not allow gelatin to return to a solid. Proceed with whipping of cream and slowly pour gelatin into the cream as it starts to thicken. With 2 cups heavy cream, there will be some left over to pipe through a pastry bag for decoration.

Unroll cake and spread with filling, leaving a 1-inch border on the far side. Roll cake gently and place seam side down on oblong platter. Cover loosely with foil and refrigerate.

My Mother's Buttermilk Cake

*M*y mother's special touch was to replace the icing with black or red raspberry jam between the layers and sprinkle confectioners' sugar over the top. This recipe, too, originated in Swans Down Flour's book *Cake Secrets*.

Yield: Approximately 8–10 servings

2½ cups sifted cake flour
½ teaspoon baking powder
½ teaspoon baking soda
1 teaspoon salt
1⅔ cups granulated sugar
6 ounces (1½ sticks) unsalted butter, at room temperature
¾ cup buttermilk, at room temperature
1 teaspoon vanilla
3 large eggs, unbeaten, at room temperature
½ cup black or red seedless raspberry jam
Confectioners' sugar

Preheat oven to 350 degrees. Butter two 9-inch round cake pans and line with waxed paper rounds.

Measure sifted cake flour into sifter; add baking powder, baking soda, salt, and sugar and reserve. Do not sift yet.

Place room-temperature butter in the bowl of an electric mixer. Stir butter, sift in dry ingredients, add buttermilk and vanilla, and mix until flour is dampened. Beat 2 minutes at low speed; add eggs and beat 1 minute longer.

Divide batter between the two prepared pans and bake on the middle rack of preheated oven 25 to 30 minutes, or until cake springs back when gently touched. Cool 10 minutes in pan, then loosen sides with a metal spatula and turn out onto racks to finish cooling.

Spread the jam on bottom layer, carefully place second layer on top of it, and sprinkle cake with confectioners' sugar.

PINEAPPLE UPSIDE-DOWN CAKE

*P*ineapple Upside-Down Cake is another family favorite, especially of my oldest son, Stan. This cake, too, goes back to my mother. To me, it seems like the best cake recipes do not reflect the current trends but are tried and true.

Yield: 8 servings

¼ pound (1 stick) unsalted butter, at room temperature
½ cup firmly packed light brown sugar
6 slices canned pineapple
1⅓ cups sifted cake flour
2 teaspoons baking powder
¼ teaspoon salt
¾ cup granulated sugar
1 egg, unbeaten, at room temperature
½ cup milk, at room temperature
1 teaspoon vanilla

---

continued

Preheat oven to 350 degrees.

Melt 4 tablespoons (½ stick) of the butter in an 8-inch square pan. Add brown sugar and blend well. Remove from heat. Arrange pineapple slices on sugar mixture; set aside.

Sift together flour, baking powder, salt, and granulated sugar three times. Cream remaining 4 tablespoons butter; add dry ingredients, egg, milk, and vanilla. Stir until all flour is dampened, then beat vigorously for 1 minute.

Pour batter over fruit mixture in pan. Bake 40 minutes, or until top is brown and firm to the touch. Cool cake in pan for 5 minutes, then invert on plate, let stand a minute, and remove pan.

Serve cake warm, and if desired, with whipped cream.

Between the lines: The secret of success when making Pineapple Upside-Down Cake is to make sure the milk, butter, and egg are at room temperature.

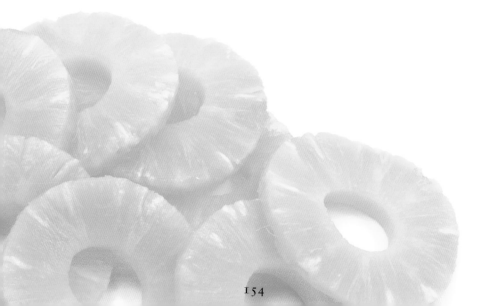

SACHERTORTE

Sachertorte originated in 1832 and was created by Viennese cook Franz Sacher, at the request of his employer, Prince Metternich. The Prince later built a hotel where the cake was served in the dining room and became world famous. Soon, many establishments in Vienna were making Sachertorte. A heated argument persisted as to the "genuine" item. At Demels, a fashionable pastry shop, the cake is made in one layer, with jam on top. At the Hotel Sacher, the cake is sliced in two. The judges voted for the Hotel Sacher's version. I, too, prefer a cake baked in one layer, but sliced horizontally and filled with apricot jam. Whatever the choice, don't forget to serve the "Schlag," or very lightly whipped best-quality cream.

Yield: 10–12 servings

6½ ounces semisweet chocolate, cut into small pieces
¼ pound (1 stick) unsalted butter
8 egg yolks
1 teaspoon vanilla extract
10 egg whites
Pinch of salt
¾ cup granulated sugar
1 cup sifted all-purpose flour
⅔ cup apricot jam, strained
Chocolate Glaze
2 cups lightly whipped cream flavored with 1 teaspoon vanilla

---

Preheat oven to 350 degrees. Butter the sides and bottom of a 10-inch round cake pan and line the bottom with parchment or waxed paper.

Combine chocolate and butter in a small pot and melt in a bain-marie (water bath), stirring occasionally. Place egg yolks in a bowl, break up with a fork, and add to chocolate-butter mixture with vanilla extract, whisking to blend ingredients.

Beat egg whites in the bowl of an electric mixer until foamy. Add salt and gradually add sugar, continuing to beat until soft peaks form. Egg whites should be stiff but not dry. Do not overbeat.

continued

Mix one-third of the egg whites into the yolk-chocolate mixture, then reverse process and fold chocolate into the rest of the whites. Sift flour over top in thirds, and continue folding with an over-and-under cutting motion, until no trace of whites or flour remains.

Pour the batter into prepared pan. Bake in the middle of the oven for 45 to 50 minutes, or until an inserted skewer comes out clean. Cool 10 minutes in pan, loosen sides with a metal spatula, and turn out on a cake rack. Remove wax paper and cool completely.

Cut the cooled cake in half horizontally. Place one layer on a cardboard cake round and spread top with apricot jam. Place second layer on top, then transfer entire cake onto a rack on top of a cookie sheet. Pour or spoon Chocolate Glaze over cake evenly, smoothing with a metal spatula if necessary. Allow cake to stand until glaze stops dripping. Refrigerate 2 to 3 hours, until glaze sets, but remove from refrigerator 30 minutes before serving. Serve with lightly whipped cream.

CHOCOLATE GLAZE

---

3 ounces unsweetened chocolate, cut into small pieces
1 cup heavy cream
1 cup sugar
1 teaspoon corn syrup
1 egg
1 teaspoon vanilla

In a small heavy saucepan, combine chocolate, cream, sugar, and corn syrup. Stirring constantly, cook on low heat until the chocolate and sugar are melted. Raise heat to medium and cook, without stirring, for 3 minutes, or until a half-teaspoon of the mixture dropped into a cup of cold water forms a soft ball.

In a small bowl, beat egg lightly, and then stir in 3 tablespoons of the chocolate. Return to remaining chocolate in saucepan, stir to combine, and cook over low heat, stirring constantly, until the glaze coats the spoon. Remove from heat, add vanilla, and cool to room temperature.

Tarte au Fromage
(French Cheesecake)

*arte au Fromage is really a delicious French cheesecake. The addition of Fromage Blanc, a French cheese similar to ricotta, adds a lightness and subtlety to the cake. I like to use my food processor—in a matter of a few minutes the cake is ready to bake. Straining the batter is not mandatory but will remove any small lumps.

Yield: 10 servings

---

1 tablespoon butter, softened
¼ cup dried breadcrumbs
¾ cup plus ½ teaspoon granulated sugar, divided
½ teaspoon cinnamon
½ pound cream cheese, at room temperature
½ pound Fromage Blanc, at room temperature (if unavailable, use all cream cheese)
4 eggs
½ cup heavy cream
1 tablespoon flour
1 teaspoon vanilla
Grated rind of 1 lemon
Confectioners' sugar
Raspberry Puree and fresh raspberries

Using the softened butter, butter an 8-inch or 9-inch springform pan well. Combine breadcrumbs, ½ teaspoon of the sugar, and cinnamon and pat into a crust on bottom and up the sides of pan.

Preheat oven to 350 degrees. Place a cookie sheet on the lower rack of the oven. Place a small pan filled with 2 cups water on the cookie sheet.

Place cream cheese and Fromage Blanc in the bowl of a food processor or an electric mixer and process or beat to blend. Add remaining ¾ cup granulated sugar. Beat until mixture is well combined and very fluffy. Add eggs one at a time, blending well after each addition. Add cream, flour, and vanilla, beating only until ingredients are combined.

continued

Strain into a clean bowl to eliminate any lumps. Add lemon rind and blend well.

Pour batter into prepared pan, wrap bottom with a piece of foil, and bake 45 minutes on middle rack of the oven, above cookie sheet and pan of water. Turn off oven, open door, and allow cheesecake to cool completely in the oven. When cool, remove sides of springform pan, sprinkle cake with confectioners' sugar, and serve with fresh raspberries and Raspberry Puree, if desired.

RASPBERRY PUREE

Yield: About ¾–1 cup sauce

---

1 package unsweetened frozen raspberries
½ cup currant or other red berry jelly
2 teaspoons cornstarch, dissolved in 1 tablespoon cold water
1 tablespoon Kirsch (optional)

Place raspberries in a small pot and mash with a wooden spoon. Add jelly and bring to a boil over low heat. Stir in dissolved cornstarch and cook, stirring, until clear. Strain and cool. Add Kirsch to cooled sauce, if desired.

OTHER

ALAN'S FAVORITE
CREAM CHEESE BROWNIES
160

BISQUE TORTONI
161

BLUEBERRY CRISP WITH
CORNMEAL CINNAMON STREUSEL
162

CHOCOLATE SOUFFLÉ
163

CLASSIC CRÈME BRÛLÉE
164

CRÈME RENVERSÉE À L'ORANGE
165

STRAWBERRY RHUBARB CRISP
166

ALAN'S FAVORITE CREAM CHEESE BROWNIES

This recipe came from the back of a package of Baker's German's Sweet Chocolate. It was a favorite when our three boys were growing up, but no one loved these brownies as much as our middle son, Alan.

Yield: About 20 brownies

One 4-ounce package Baker's German's Sweet Chocolate
5 tablespoons butter, divided
1 3-ounce package cream cheese
1 cup granulated sugar, divided
3 eggs
½ cup plus 1 tablespoon all-purpose flour, divided
1½ teaspoons vanilla, divided
½ teaspoon baking powder
¼ teaspoon salt
½ cup lightly toasted blanched almonds, chopped
¼ teaspoon almond extract
Confectioners' sugar (optional)

Melt chocolate and 3 tablespoons of the butter in a small pot over very low heat, stirring to combine. Cool.

In the bowl of an electric mixer, cream remaining 2 tablespoons butter with cream cheese and beat until light. Gradually add ¼ cup of the sugar, beating well. Stir in 1 egg, 1 tablespoon of the flour, and ½ teaspoon of the vanilla and blend well. Set aside.

Beat remaining 2 eggs until light and pale in color. Gradually add remaining ¾ cup sugar and beat until thick. Gently beat in baking powder, salt, and remaining ½ cup flour, mixing well. Add chocolate mixture, nuts, almond extract, and remaining 1 teaspoon vanilla. Blend mixture well.

Preheat oven to 350 degrees. Grease a 9-inch square pan.

Using two large spoons, drop dollops of chocolate and cream cheese mixtures, making a checkerboard pattern. With a knife, zigzag through batter to marble.

Bake approximately 40 minutes, until top is lightly browned and sides pull away from the pan. Cool. Cut into squares and, if desired, sprinkle with confectioners' sugar.

Bisque Tortoni

Yield: 10–12 servings

---

1 cup crumbled Amaretti macaroons
1 tablespoon Kirsch or Grand Marnier liqueur
1 cup heavy cream
3 tablespoons Framboise or Grand Marnier liqueur
1 quart vanilla ice cream
½ cup blanched almonds, toasted and chopped
1 ounce (1 square) bittersweet chocolate, grated

In a small bowl, sprinkle macaroon crumbs with Kirsch or Grand Marnier and set aside.

Whip cream until stiff and beat in the Framboise or Grand Marnier. Refrigerate until needed.

Soften ice cream in the large bowl of an electric mixer or with a wooden spoon. Fold in whipped cream, almonds, chocolate, and macaroon crumbs, blending well. Turn the mixture into foil-lined paper cupcake cups and freeze until firm, about 4 hours. If desired, use some extra nuts, macaroon crumbs, or chocolate as a topping.

BLUEBERRY CRISP WITH CORNMEAL CINNAMON STREUSEL

Crisps are versatile and easy to do and provide the perfect homemade dessert. Cornmeal adds crunch and texture and an interesting contrast to luscious summer blueberries.

Yield: 10 servings

6 cups blueberries
3 tablespoons granulated sugar
Grated rind of 1 lemon
1 teaspoon lemon juice
Pinch of salt

Preheat oven to 400 degrees. Butter a 2-quart shallow baking or gratin dish.

In a large bowl, combine blueberries, sugar, lemon rind, lemon juice, and salt. Turn into prepared baking dish.

STREUSEL TOPPING

½ cup firmly packed light brown sugar
1 teaspoon cinnamon
½ cup unbleached all-purpose flour
½ cup yellow cornmeal
¼ pound (1 stick) cold unsalted butter, cut into dice

In a large bowl, combine light brown sugar, cinnamon, flour, and cornmeal. Using a pastry blender, cut butter into dry ingredients, making large crumbs. Sprinkle over blueberries and bake 35 to 40 minutes, or until fruit is bubbly and streusel topping lightly browned.

Serve Crisp warm with ice cream, frozen yogurt, or whipped cream, if desired.

Chocolate Soufflé

I learned how to make chocolate soufflé from Madeleine Kamman when I was one of her students in Annecy, France. Madeleine Kamman is an extraordinary chef and teacher and an outstanding writer. As a teacher and friend, she influenced me greatly and taught me not only the art of fine cooking but about her native country.

Yield: 8 servings

8 egg yolks
½ cup sugar, divided
Pinch of salt
2 teaspoons powdered instant coffee, or 2 tablespoons brewed coffee
3 tablespoons cognac or dark rum
8 ounces bittersweet chocolate, cut into small pieces
¼ cup heavy cream
10 egg whites

Use 8 individual soufflé molds. Butter each and sprinkle with sugar, turning upside down to remove excess.

Beat egg yolks with 5 tablespoons of the sugar, until yolks are light and lemon-colored. Add a pinch of salt, coffee, and cognac or rum and beat again.

Melt chocolate in a small pan in a water bath. Cool slightly and blend into yolks, alternating with cream.

Beat egg whites until soft shapes form, and then gradually beat in remaining 3 tablespoons sugar. Mix about one-quarter of the beaten whites into the chocolate to lighten, then fold chocolate into the rest of the whites. Turn into prepared molds, filling three-quarters full. Place molds on a cookie sheet and bake on the bottom rack of the oven for approximately 15 minutes, or until soufflés have puffed and crusted on top.

Serve with whipped cream, chilled Crème Anglaise, or a dollop of vanilla ice cream. To do this, use a spoon to make a hole in the center of the soufflé and add the topping. The contrast between hot and cold is delightful.

continued

Between the lines: It is possible to prepare the soufflés ahead and freeze them in their dishes. When frozen, cover with plastic wrap or tin foil. When ready to use, preheat the oven to 400 degrees. Remove soufflés from the freezer and allow them to defrost for 20 to 30 minutes. Bake 15 minutes, or until puffed with a light crust on top.

CLASSIC CRÈME BRÛLÉE

Yield: 10–12 servings

1 cup granulated sugar, divided
1 quart heavy cream
1-inch piece of vanilla bean
10 egg yolks, graded large
½ cup raw sugar

Preheat oven to 325 degrees.

Combine ½ cup of the sugar, heavy cream, and vanilla bean in a pot. Bring to a boil, remove from heat, and allow bean to steep in cream 30 minutes.

Place yolks in the bowl of an electric mixer. At medium speed, gradually add remaining ½ cup sugar. Increase speed and beat until mixture ribbons (or falls back on itself when beaters are lifted). Add ½ cup of the cream to egg yolk mixture, incorporating by stirring, and then gently add remaining cream, stirring well to combine. Do not whisk or beat mixture, because it will cause air bubbles. Pass custard through a fine strainer and divide among ramekins, small soufflé dishes, or custard cups, allowing approximately ⅓ to ½ cup per dish.

Place ramekins in shallow roasting pan. Pour enough hot water to come slightly less than halfway up sides of ramekins and bake approximately 30 minutes, until custard is set around the edges but still loose in the middle. Cool in water bath, then refrigerate, loosely covered with plastic wrap, for at least 2 hours or overnight.

To serve: Sprinkle tops evenly with raw sugar (2 to 3 teaspoons each), then melt sugar with a hand torch or under the broiler. Serve immediately.

CRÈME RENVERSÉE À L'ORANGE

On our first trip to Cannes as a family, we frequently dined at restaurants, but not at the starred restaurants listed in the Michelin Guide. We chose bistros and small restaurants on the waterfront where meals could be reasonably ordered complete. Inevitably, one of the desserts was always Crème Caramel, which soon became a family favorite. Here is an orange-flavored version.

Yield: 8 servings

CARAMEL

1 cup granulated sugar
½ cup water
Few drops of lemon juice

Preheat oven to 350 degrees. Fill a large pan with enough water to come halfway up the sides and place in the oven.

Place sugar and water in a heavy saucepan. Add lemon juice and cook over moderately high heat until mixture has caramelized. Do not stir. Color of caramel should be a deep amber.

Moving quickly and carefully, cover the bottom of eight ½-cup custard or soufflé dishes with a layer of hot caramel. Set aside.

CUSTARD

2 cups milk
½ cup sugar
Grated rind of 1 orange (include no white pith)
1 teaspoon vanilla, or 1 small piece of vanilla bean
3 whole eggs
3 egg yolks
2 tablespoons Grand Marnier liqueur

continued

Pour milk into a saucepan. Add sugar, grated orange rind, and vanilla or vanilla bean. Cook over low heat, stirring, until milk comes to a full boil.

Break eggs into a bowl. Add egg yolks and whisk together. Pour the boiled milk into the egg mixture, whisking all the time. Pass through a fine strainer into a pitcher. Add Grand Marnier and divide mixture among caramel-lined custard cups. Place in a bain-marie (water bath) and bake 25 minutes. Check to see if a skewer inserted into custard comes out clean. If so, remove from oven and allow custards to cool in water bath. Remove custards by loosening sides with a small metal spatula and turning out onto a plate. Serve at room temperature. Custards may also be served cold, but in that case, do not remove from baking cups until ready to use.

Strawberry Rhubarb Crisp

When I first introduced this recipe in my cooking classes, I was actually embarrassed because it was so easy. I was surprised and delighted by the positive feedback. Not only did the class like the Crisp, but everyone went home and made it. To this day, people still tell me Strawberry Rhubarb Crisp was their favorite cooking class recipe.

Yield: 10 servings

Fruit

6 tablespoons granulated sugar
2 tablespoons all-purpose flour
Dash of salt
1 teaspoon cinnamon
2 cups rhubarb, peeled, trimmed of ends, and cut into ¾–1-inch pieces
1½ pints ripe strawberries, hulled and cut in half

Combine granulated sugar, flour, salt, and cinnamon in a large bowl and mix well. Add rhubarb and strawberries and toss fruit and dry mixture together until evenly coated. Place fruit in a large, shallow gratin or baking dish and cover evenly with topping.

TOPPING

1 cup slivered almonds, lightly toasted (I use a toaster oven)
1 cup all-purpose flour
1 cup firmly packed light brown sugar
⅛ teaspoon salt
¼ pound (1 stick) cold unsalted butter, cut into dice

Chop cooled almonds coarsely. Combine the flour, brown sugar, salt, and almonds in a mixing bowl. With a pastry blender or your fingers, incorporate butter while keeping the topping textured and crumbly.

Preheat oven to 400 degrees.

Sprinkle topping evenly over fruit and bake 45 minutes, until brown, bubbly, and crisp.

Serve warm with excellent-quality vanilla ice cream or whipped cream, if desired.

ACKNOWLEDGMENTS

Special thanks to Karen Mugler, whose help and patience with this book was very much appreciated.

Also, thanks to the people at CPI Creative who worked so diligently to put this together in a relatively short period of time and did such a beautiful job designing it.

Last, but certainly not least, thank you to Carl for graciously stepping forward to support this project. All we can say is, Jane would be pleased.

SUSAN AND ALAN CITRON